Canals, Canines and Curry

Michael I. Rolfe

Published by Accent Press Ltd – 2014

ISBN 9781783755967

For my beautiful fiancée Cat, a BIG thank you for the idea!

Also my thanks to Stanley; for the dog hair, the drool, the snoring, the scratches on the walls, mess around your food bowl, the odd "little accident", and for just being a big lovable dog!

A new boaters' perspective of life on the inland waterways – an informative and occasionally humorous look at a couple and their colossal canine; charting their learning curve from calamitous collisions through to confident competence, all fuelled by copious curries.

Photos by Cat Lee

FOREWORD

They say boredom is powerful. A sensation which has driven many individuals to act away from the norm.

Born out of boredom – could this explain how it all started?

I had to undergo major surgery and I knew I was going to be confined to bed convalescing for at least a couple of months. For someone of my active nature this was going to be a frustrating time. There was not much else to do but resign myself to my melancholy and try to see the positives in the situation: one of them would be the joys of being waited on hand and foot by my man!

There is only a limited number of activities that anyone can do in an incapacitated state: sleep, sleep, and more sleep, watch TV. Sleep again and read in bed.

In preparation for the boredom to come, a week before I was due for admission into hospital I had ordered a few books online. A couple of these were on the topic of canals and boats.

Two weeks prior to my surgery, on a cold winter morning I had been out watching the Severn Bore, a large intermittent tidal wave that runs up the River Severn, I had stopped afterwards for coffee at The Wharf House in Over near Gloucester.

It was my first visit to The Wharf House. On entering the reception area I was instantly drawn to the impressive colourful plaque that spanned an entire wall detailing the Herefordshire & Gloucestershire Canal, in an otherwise plain contemporary decor.

Leaflets and books, all forms of literature about the canal and boats, were displayed in orderly fashion around the seating areas. They were difficult to ignore.

I sat inside though they had a pretty terrace overlooking the river. I made a mental note to try it on a warmer day. I had placed my derriere onto the deep comfy sofa and ordered a coffee and hot buttered croissant. Immersing myself in canal boats literature and sipping my hot full-bodied beverage, my imagination started to get carried away.

I started to image how much fun it would be to have a boat. I imagined eating strawberries and cream sitting on the bow deck and heartily blowing my saxophone as we cruised down the river. And Christmas on a boat, now that would be novel!

Being gently rocked to sleep and waking up to the dawn mist. How about sipping wine and watching the stars with Ken Watanabe lying on the roof of the boat. See what I mean about my imagination getting carried away!

I left The Wharf House that day with a warm happy feeling inside from having a grandiose idea.

With hindsight, perhaps the seed had already been planted five years before when we were at Neptune's Staircase near Fort William. We had visited it on one of our leisurely sightseeing days before setting out to climb Ben Nevis from the arduous north route.

Neptune's Staircase is an impressive sight consisting of a set of eight locks. The canal rises 64 feet in 450yards. A clever canal engineering feat with nothing else like it at the time it was built.

The idea of owning a boat was not shared with my man until a few days after I got back home from the operation when I started to read my books.

Over the years my man has had to put up with and hear a myriad of my crazy ideas.

My enthusiasm for them has been short-lived on many occasions. My man has effortless ability in pointing out all the impracticalities. But it has never crushed my natural inquisitive nature or put me off from germinating new ideas!

On this occasion it took a couple of days before he started to warm to the splendour of it all.

I told him that, if we were to buy a boat, it would be the following year – allowing us time to save up. So much for that!

His reasoning was life is too short to wait and summer was coming.

When my man likes an idea and gets it into his head, there is utterly no way of stopping him! He can crystallize an idea and turn it into reality faster than Mike Tyson can win his first round!

We have had sleepless nights since our offer for a boat was accepted. At bedtimes it has been a case of man planning the practical logistic side of getting it home and woman thinking about furnishing (more important of course!) and planning our Christmas onboard.

Despite being sleep-deprived we walk around these days with a permanent smile both inside and out. As for Stanley, the dog, he is not any wiser. He is happy as long as he gets his walks although I have noticed a few bemused perplexed head tilts and tail wags as his mum and dad go about the day in a more happy-go-lucky way than usual.

Our path in the future has suddenly branched out and taken a whole new direction.

The thought is immensely exciting! But …

In a few days my man, accompanied by friends, will embark on the maiden voyage to bring our boat safely back home. A group of men together equates to mischief and trouble even in the most normal of circumstances. Most notably none of these men has any practical boat skills or handling experience! Mike with his one week self-taught book theory. His actual boat course is not for two weeks.

A group of men and one dog the size of a small donkey in a confined space – it's going to be cosy! On a boat that they know only in theory how to operate and with gas cylinders, petrol, water and matches. What could possibly go wrong?

I lay in bed at home with my knuckles in my mouth and my stomach churning with worry. Our boat was doomed!

Cat Lee

Recuperative Research

It all started because Cat, my fiancée, had been reading a lot; she was recovering from a major operation so this was a preferable alternative to watching the TV or staring up at the ceiling. One of the books was titled *Narrow Margins*, and was about a couple who had given up their jobs, sold their house, and moved their family onto a narrowboat. Cat and I started to take it in turns to read their story to each other and when I returned from work at the end of each day I would ask Cat to update me on their latest exploits.

I have always liked campervans – the idea of having a home from home that is mobile has always appealed to me – and a boat with bed, sink, and cooker etc. that could cruise around the waterways appealed to both of us. The whole idea of a slower life away from work, colleagues, bosses, and the rat-race in general, sounded wonderful. If only I could win the lottery, I could really start to live my life for me: being able to have an unhurried morning walk with Stanley, our dog; not having to jump into the car, endure the congestion on the drive to work, and then rush back home afterwards.

To be honest, I really have had enough of my job, but I am realistic enough to know that I am not brave enough to take the plunge, give it all up, and buy, then live on, a boat ... not now ... not yet ... but the idea was, and still is, appealing. I did not want to let the dream of freedom die.

So I thought: why not at least look into it? I could find out what boats and a life on the water are like. So, with thoughts of a better, less stressful future existence, I turned on the computer and started my research into the craft that cruise the inland waterways of the UK.

One of the first things I learned is that if you want to cruise the whole of the canal and river network (over three thousand miles of it) you will need a boat that has a beam (width) of no more than 6' 10": so I would be looking for a narrowboat! Then there was the air draft (height) to consider – this is not so straightforward but in general if you can keep the height below 6' 5" you should be able to go most places. There are some low bridges, tunnels, and culverts on the canal network! Then there was the length to contemplate; narrowboats can be up to 70 foot, so how long should our boat be? The length would depend, I realised, on how many people would be on the vessel and how long they were going to spend there. Another thing to decide was the type of hull (underside of the boat), was it to be wood, steel, aluminium, or GRP (glass reinforced plastic, also known as fibreglass)? One of the last things to think about was the cost, and therein lay the rub! How much one is prepared to spend on a boat will dictate to a large degree one's decisions on these things.

I also found out that the longer and wider the boat, the more it costs, not just to buy it in the first place, but also the cost of mooring, maintenance, and the annual river and canal licences.

Estimates of the cost of maintenance also vary depending on the type of hull (and who you talk to!) A boat with a steel hull should be taken out of the water every three years or so to have the hull examined and re-blackened. Re-blackening involves lifting the boat via a crane, or utilising a dry dock, then pressure-washing the underside and sometime scraping the hull clean – even back to the bare metal – then recovering it with bitumen hull-blacking paint. Steel boats will also need their sacrificial anodes checking and possibly replacing. Basically, without getting too deeply into the science of the thing, the idea is that any galvanic currents around the boat will be attracted to the anode and away from the steel hull of the boat, so the anode will then slowly erode instead of the hull.

Glass reinforced plastic boats tend not to need so much hull maintenance; but they are not so resilient to the inevitable knocks that happen as you cruise the inland waterways. GRP craft will still need to be taken out of the water occasionally to have the hull examined, cleaned/rubbed down, and repainted with antifouling paint.

After much research, I came to the conclusion that living on a boat is relatively cheap but living in a house and having a boat as a "toy" is just the opposite! We really needed to think what we would use the boat for, and why did we actually want it?

After a lot of thought and many discussions, Cat and I decided that we were not going to live on a boat to start with; it was not practical for us as we had work and Stanley, our rather large Akita dog.

Akitas are a Spitz-type breed (think large, Husky-like dog) originally from Japan. They are very strong, powerful, independent, and dominant animals. To give you some idea of just how powerful this breed is: Akitas were used for hunting wild boar, deer, and bears in Japan; they would chase and then hold a bear at bay until the human hunters could administer the *coup de grâce*.

Stanley is a large example of an Akita, he weighs over 52 kg, and being an Akita can be a bit of a handful. Living in our house (which is basically a large kennel!) he has the run of the place and unfettered access to the totally enclosed garden of our modest end-terrace house. Being able to please himself when/if he needs to go into the garden is great for him when we are out at work. If we were to live onboard a boat he would not have this luxury.

Stanley and I at Sharpness

With this in mind, it was back to the computer and, with a rough idea of what we were looking for, I started to trawl through the myriad of boats that were for sale at various boat brokerage sites.

With a new interest in the local waterways and the boats upon them, I took to walking Stanley along the River Severn, though the Gloucester Docks, and onto the Gloucester & Sharpness Canal. I was now looking at the boats with a semi-educated eye; I could now tell the difference between a cruiser, a barge, a narrowboat, and the more subtle variations that there are among the narrowboats themselves. The main difference is at the stern (rear of the boat); there are basically three popular types of narrowboat: traditional (or "trad"), semi trad or cruiser stern. Traditional narrowboats have a very small rear deck which only really has room for the person steering the boat and perhaps one other crew member; a cruiser stern has a much larger deck with room for up to four or five people, while a semi trad is a cross between the two.

On one walk I stopped and had a chat with the keeper at Gloucester Lock. Feeling a bit like an imposter because I did not even own a boat, I asked him about the River Severn, his lock, and local moorings. He was very helpful and did not mind at all that I was asking speculative questions.

A month and hundreds of boat searches later, I was ready to take a look at my first boat; a 30-foot river cruiser/narrowboat hybrid that was moored at Ashwood Marina. Cat was still recovering from her operation and was not well enough to make the trip so she stayed at home while I drove up to Ashwood to see the boat and reported back. It should be said at this stage that I was just going to look and had no intention of buying anything!

First Impressions Don't Count

It was a quick drive up the motorway in our VW campervan to Ashwood. And it was with some excitement that I walked along the waterside looking at the dozens of boats moored alongside the linear marina. Some boats were for sale, some lived in, and others were moored waiting for their owners to play with them on the weekend. I was shown to the boat by a lady broker who was also the marina owner.

At first glance the vessel looked OK, in fact pretty good. I stepped up on the stern deck and this is where my initial estimation of her (the boat not the broker) started to diminish. The steering wheel was a ship-type and one of the spars had been snapped off. Descending down the two steep steps into the main cabin my initial impression was reduced further still. It was grubby and a half-hearted attempt had been made to refurbish the interior. The taps were missing and half the curtains and some of the curtain rails were also gone. The roof lining looked like it had been stuck to the ceiling by a paralytic pigmy on a pogo-stick, and the green paint that adorned the cupboard doors looked like it was chosen and then smeared on by a homesick extra-terrestrial, I was not impressed! I spent a few more minutes poking around and finding other minor horrors before disembarking. To be fair, the description in the advertisement had not been far from the reality, in an estate agent kind of way.

As we walked back to the office I asked the broker

about another craft that was for sale in the marina, and so it was that I looked at my second ever boat. This one was very nice, it was a mid-cockpit cruiser and well presented inside and out, but, given the layout, not that practical for Stanley to get in and out of. It was at this time when it dawned on me the first boat, the one that had been renovated by a colour-blind short-sighted zombie with a nervous tick, would be perfect!

I drove home and as the miles ticked by I hatched a plan. I knew that although Cat had come up with the original idea to own a boat she was not ready to buy one just yet; she wanted to wait until the following year. This was of course the sensible thing to do. I, on the other hand, had seen the now "perfect" boat. I was keen to get on with the job of fixing it up – after of course sorting out the minor problems of persuading Cat to go for it, negotiating with the owner to drop the price by a nautical mile, and getting the money together! I was a man on a mission. As I pulled Brian, our campervan, (yes, it does have a name) onto our drive, my plan was complete. Now it was time for implementation!

I ran upstairs to reveal to Cat the unquestionable logic that had led me to the conclusion that we should buy a boat as yet unseen by her, with that special paint job inside, oh, and did I mention that nothing other than the engine worked?

Cat could see that my logic was incontestable, however, for a reason known only to herself, she felt compelled to explain to me in simple terms her own (which she considered unquestionable) reasons why we should NOT buy the perfect (OK, almost perfect) boat.

After an hour of debate, the undeniable brilliance of my logic won the day and we were ready to put in a ridiculous offer (we had nothing to lose). The broker was duly called and the offer was made.

Stanley was now well overdue a walk, so I was

despatched up the local hill, lead in hand, to be dragged through thorny flora by a pent-up dog with the strength of a shire horse. As I was attempting to maintain a vertical stance while trying not to twist an ankle following Stanley, my mobile telephone rang. It was the broker with an answer from her client: our offer had been rejected.

In truth the rejection of the offer was no surprise; this was all part of the master plan (I told myself), so now; as I stood on top of a hill on a beautifully sunny afternoon early in the month of April with Stanley sat at my side, I put in a final offer for the boat that was perfect for us.

Stanley finished his walk and other associated business and, after clearing up after him, we returned home for dinner. It was while food was being prepared (yes, I did wash my hands) that we got the call informing us that us our second offer had been accepted.

Arrangements were made to meet the owner the following weekend for a "sea trial" (a trip on the canal) in the boat to make sure all was well, then, assuming we were happy, we could then go ahead with the purchase.

I hung up the phone and looked at Cat with an uncertain smile on my face. I think we were both a bit shocked with the pace at which things were going and the enormity of what we were about to do! I said, 'Well, that's it, if all goes well we should have our own boat in a few weeks!'

She said excitedly, 'Oh what have we done?'

To which I replied uncertainly, 'Let's not worry about that, let's just enjoy the moment!' We sat down to our meal excitedly making plans for what would be a new chapter in our lives. I'm not sure what Stanley made of all this excited chatter, but he eyed our food with hopeful anticipation.

The following week – as with all working weeks – dragged by with the speed of a three-legged tortoise who had been told to take it easy by his cardiologist. Saturday eventually arrived and it was at last time to look at the boat again. I had enlisted the help of Dave H., a long-term friend, to come and see the boat. Also, should the sale go ahead, he would help me cruise her home. Dave H. is a talented guitarist (mainly rocky blues) but this was not the reason he was coming to the marina with me; he had driven a speedboat once before while on holiday, so that made him the expert on all things nautical. It really was a question of the near-sighted leading the blind.

After a quick trip up the motorway, we walked to where the boat was moored and were introduced to the owner, who showed us around the boat again. For some reason it did not seem so bad this time, now that I was seeing the potential and not just the existing state of affairs. I could now visualise the interior with a new coat of paint, blinds replacing the remaining curtains, and with the new seats with storage, which would convert into a large double bed, that I was planning to build in the front of the cabin.

After the second tour of the boat the owner was to take us on our sea trial. He was also going to show us how to work the canal locks and give some advice on the finer points of boating. Then he reversed out of the marina, hitting nearly every moored boat in the process. 'Wind,' explained the owner, 'makes it difficult to steer at slow speed.' I was not sure what flatulence had to do with operating a boat, but I was a total novice, so I made a mental note and wondered just how well my favourite food (curry) and boating would go together ...

Once we had cleared the marina, and the bobbing vessels had resettled on their mooring ropes, the owner selected forward gear and we advanced northwards along the Staffordshire & Worcestershire Canal. The first thing I noticed was that we were driving on the "wrong side of the road". It turns out that you drive (cruise) on the right-hand side on the waterway; this would take some getting used to!

This was my first trip on any canal and I wanted to savour the experience, but almost as soon as we were underway I was invited over to the wheel to take control. How hard can it be? I thought to myself.

I hesitantly took hold of the helm and managed to keep the vessel in a straight line for approximately five seconds before it started to veer to starboard (that's nautical for right); I swung the wheel over to port (yes, you guessed it, that's left) and then continued down the canal like a crazed pinball in a slow-motion mission to hit the bank more times than a pugilist would hit a punchbag. I was not having fun! So, as it turns out, steering a canal boat is not that easy to start with, and I thought that perhaps boating and I were not really well suited.

I would only realise later that I was over-correcting by throwing the wheel from one side to the other in a vain attempt to go in a straight line. But at the time I continued to zigzag along the canal. Happily for me, Dave wanted to have a go at the helm and I soon realised that he was better at navigating the water than me.

We moored before the first of the two locks that we were going to negotiate, then were shown how to operate the paddles and gates; this was my first time in a lock – it was a pleasant experience. At the next lock Dave and I operated it without any mishaps, so it transpired that canal locks and I are at least are compatible.

On the return trip I was to steer the boat through the smaller gaps under the bridges and in the locks; this caused me a fair amount apprehension but I did manage to guide the bow and, in turn, the stern through with no more than a little scrape. However, this was only achieved by concentrating as if I was gliding the space shuttle into land with no computer assistance. I was still not having fun!

When we arrived back at Ashwood we decided that the boat would be reversed back through the linear marina to her berth so that she would be facing in the correct direction for her next cruise. I thought this was a good idea until it was determined that I should be the one who did the reversing. So, with awful visions of destroying most of the boats at their mooring, I took the wheel, selected reverse, and cruised backwards through the small channel between the moored boats. Without hitting anything! I was looking like an old hand of the waterways, which I certainly was not.

With my confidence partly restored, the sale of one cruiser/narrowboat hybrid was agreed. It was followed by the first batch of what would turn out to be a lot of paperwork and organising to be done.

To avoid having to take too many days off of work, I wanted to bring our new acquisition home over the first weekend in May, which happened to be a bank holiday, but this only left me two weeks to get everything organised. I thought I had done all the research and knew what to expect, however, not for the first or last time theory would prove no match for reality. The list of tasks never seems to get shorter; I would enquire about one thing only to be told that I would need something else first. It was not looking good and I feared our schedule would slip. Some things went well: the bank transfer of the funds for the boat went through and Dave H. said he would be able to help me cruise the boat back. However, I could not get the canal and river licence without the boat safety certificate, but this took time to be sent to me, I would also need insurance to get the licence but, because the boat was over 25 years old, I would need a full out-of-the-water survey and there was no way that could be done in time. Even finding a marina to leave the boat in was not that straightforward; I left four messages over an eight-day period at one marina office before I was finally called back, only to be told that they had no space available (the pace of communication and work takes place at the same speed as canal transit at that particular marina). It seemed to be that the whole thing was an enormous Catch-22. After an inordinate amount work, wheeling, dealing, and jumping through lots of hoops, everything was finally completed just in time.

Akita and the Staffordshire & Worcestershire Canal

And so it was on one sunny Thursday afternoon before the bank holiday weekend, Stanley, Dave H., and I found ourselves travelling back up to the marina for the final time to collect our boat. Noel, my mum's partner, was to drive our campervan back from Ashwood and leave it at Saul Junction, our new marina.

In addition to the boring paperwork side of things, I had spent weeks preparing for the cruise from Ashwood Marina back to Gloucester, in fact I had started even before I had signed on the dotted line to make the boat ours. A list of items to cover every eventuality short of a Zombie outbreak had been drawn up and lots of toys for the boat had been ordered, including an anchor that would not have been out of place on an oil tanker. I had been studying the *Waterways Guide Number 2 (Severn, Avon & Birmingham)* so I knew the route well (in theory) and I had also been reading the RYA (Royal Yachting Association) *Inland Waterways Handbook*. I had even booked myself on a boat-handling course, but events had overtaken me and now I would be cruising my own boat home weeks before the course. (Great timing Mike!)

So I had a list of everything we would need for a four-day cruise home (in theory), I had acquired everything one could possibly need on a boat for the trip home (in theory) and I knew all there was to know about boating on the inland waterways (in theory). There would be two humans, a dog the size of a small horse, petrol, gas, water, lots of curry, and we would be in a confined space on a boat that we only knew in theory how to operate. What could possibly go wrong?

The equipment, Stanley, and all the theory were loaded into our VW campervan, then some of the kit had to be unloaded and abandoned to make way for the crew.

In the van the drive from our home in Gloucester to Ashwood Marina (situated not too far north of Kidderminster) took just over an hour, the cruise back would take us four days; travel on our inland waterways does not take place at light speed!

The drive was uneventful and we arrived at the marina around mid afternoon. While Dave took Stanley for a walk to do his ablutions, I, with the help of the now ex-owner of the boat and his friend, unloaded the vast amount of baggage from the van and into the boat (I think the van breathed a sigh of relief once the weight of the anchor and chain was removed). Upon Dave and Stanley's return (Stanley now also a little lighter) we started the engine and moved the boat down to the water point to fill up.

Once the water jerrycans were filled, we started our cruise home. Dave took first shift at the wheel, but Steve the ex-owner and his friend were cruising with us for the first part of the trip and they worked the locks, leaving me to sort out the boat and look after Stanley.

Encouraged by Steve, we cruised along at a pace that was perhaps a bit too fast and we upset the occupants of at least one moored boat. I did not like this and felt that I was not really in control of the situation or the boat, and was looking forward to the time that Steve and Co. would disembark leaving myself, Dave, and Stanley to our own devices. As evening arrived we reached the place where I had planned to moor for the night: Kinver. Being new to boating I was not sure where we were allowed to moor. I shouldn't have worried, the visitor moorings were well signposted and there was plenty of room alongside the towpath. We shook hands with the Steve and he and his friend departed to the pub; now at last, and for the first time, both Dave and I felt that we could relax and start to enjoy the trip as masters of our own destiny and the boat.

Dave was despatched to acquire the first curry of the trip; and as Stanley had been on the boat for a while he took me for a walk, dragging me along the towpath and leaving his calling card for other dogs to sniff at a later date. We all arrived back at the boat for our spicy cuisine. Once fed, watered, and after Stanley had taken me out for a last wee, it was time to settle down for our first ever night on a boat. With thoughts of waking up knee-deep in canal water I attempted to drift off to sleep.

As we were settling down for the night I said to Dave, 'Oh, I forgot to tell you, Stanley may snore a bit'. OK so "may snore a bit" may have been misleading on the same scale as Tony Blair's statement about weapons of mass destruction, but I did not want to spoil the sheer delight, nay the sheer shock and awe, that Dave would experience once he was subjected to Stanley's snoring. To give you some idea as to the majesty of the sound that Stanley can emit once he has trotted off to doggy dreamland, just think along the lines of a Motörhead gig taking place during a hurricane and real weapons of mass destruction detonating all at the same time! I also had to mention to Dave about Stanley's "slight" tendency to run in his sleep, this meant that his claws would be drumming and scratching on any surface that came to paw, and then there is his propensity to break wind. Did I mention we all had curry that evening?

By the following morning, I think Dave was suitably impressed and maybe just a little shell-shocked! Never mind, Dave, only two nights to go …

Now would be a good time to tell you just a little more about our new "perfect" boat: nothing worked! Well the engine did run quite well but the battery was flat so there was a bit of old rope that we were meant use to pull-start the engine, however, one of the many items that I had brought with us was a backup "booster battery" so at least we could connect this and start the engine with the key. The horn, tunnel light, and internal lights did not work so we had a hand-held spotlight and head torches. There was no running water, so we had jerrycans on the foredeck, to which we had to make countless trips to fill the kettle for our numerous mugs of tea (tea on a canal boat seems to be a prerequisite); fortunately the gas hob did work!

Internally the cabin had potential but lots of work would be required to realise it. The front of the cabin was open-plan, this is where I was trying to sleep, but there were two chairs situated in this area that just kept getting in the way – the thought of throwing them overboard did cross my mind a few times. The chairs were stacked on top of each other to minimise the floor space they took up. Cat, after seeing them in the photos, had taken a liking to them and they were destined for use in her study at home. On a smallish boat anything the size of those chairs would have to be dual-purpose i.e. chairs by day, bed by night, and if you could store stuff in them, so much the better!

So Cat was to get her wish; both chairs had to be disassembled just to get them out of the narrow bow doors.

Back from the open-plan front cabin the galley was situated along the starboard side starting with the cooker and hob, counter space with cupboards (with door which would not open) leading on to a drainer and medium-size sink (with taps which did not flow). Continuing from the sink there was more counter space with a non-functioning gas boiler above. On the port side was a diner which could seat four but the brackets to hold up the table were missing so the table top, which also makes the diner seats into a bed (this is where Dave was bunked), was stored in the non-functioning shower room situated back from the diner on the port side.

The all-important and thankfully operational toilet was left on the redundant shower tray in the shower room where it would have been nice to be able to wash your hands in the, yes, you guessed it, permanently dry sink.

Further back from the waterless shower there were two small bunks; any person reclining in them would have their legs stretching under the rear deck. I think all previous owners must have been claustrophobic because the plastic covers were still in place on the mattresses after twenty-five years. Not being that practical or desirable as beds, the spaces were soon full of all the gear that we had brought with us; the port side "bunk" serving as a location for our 12-volt fridge. When, much later, we finally cleared the junk from the bunk on the starboard side, Stanley jumped in to the newly freed-up bed space and made it his own!

Two very steep steps led up to the rear deck behind/above the "bunks" and this is where the boat is operated from. There is a "pram cover" (soft-top foldable roof) over the rear deck to keep the rain and sun off. Right at the stern of the boat and stretching from port to starboard is a large seat, the seat cover of which can be lifted to expose the engine, gas, and battery lockers.

The list of what needed doing on the boat read like the Domesday Book; I was to have a lot of work to do in the near, and as it turned out, not-so-near future and with every mile we cruised nearer to home the list of unserviceable items and the cost to fix them grew! That said I did know that the boat was far from faultless and this was reflected in the final price paid, the main thing was that I did not wake up the following morning knee-deep in canal water!

We had renamed our boat "*Akita*" after the breed of our dog, Stanley.

Akita's vital statistics are:

30′ (9 m 14 cm) in length

Beam of 6'10" (2 m 8 cm)

Draft (approximately) 1' (35 cm)

Air Draft (height above the water) 6' 9" (2 m 5cm)

You need to know this stuff if you are going the cruise the inland waterways and you will be asked about some of the above on occasion by lock-keepers and marinas, etc.

Akita is a cruiser/narrowboat hybrid, the hull is GRP, and she was built by Highbridge Cruisers in 1988. The current engine is a Yamaha 9.9HP (4 stroke petrol inboard/outboard). Like a normal narrowboat *Akita* is steered from a deck at the stern (rear of the boat) but a wheel is used rather than using a tiller to operate the rudder/engine.

We woke the following morning – well Stanley woke up, neither Dave nor I had slept much (thank you, Stanley) but we were still afloat so we were off to a good start.

We had breakfast and prepared to cast off. Dave was going to "drive" the boat and I was to walk Stanley along the towpath and work the locks. I pushed *Akita* away from the bank, Dave engaged gear, and the engine stalled, leaving Dave drifting in the middle of the canal. Another lesson learnt: LET THE ENGINE WARM UP! Dave threw a rope and I pulled *Akita* back to the bank. We lifted the engine bay cover, reconnected the booster battery, and started her up again, and this time cast off with no problems.

The weather was great, not a cloud in the sky, and it was a nice feeling to be walking Stanley the Akita dog down the towpath alongside *Akita* the boat, towards the first lock that I would operate on my own. Whittington Lock is in a beautiful setting, giving you a real "olde worlde" feeling. To my relief the lock was negotiated with ease, we then continued under Whittington Bridge and south along the "Cut" (canal).

The Staffordshire & Worcestershire Canal was opened circa 1772. Things (and people) must have been smaller then; it was a real tight fit in some of the locks and you have to squeeze the boat through some of the bridges. In fact on some occasions you have to duck if you're standing on the stern deck steering the boat. On this my maiden voyage, due to my lack of confidence or any skill, I did not like the fact that some of the spaces that I was expected to guide our boat through were so minute. I resented the original builders for making things so tight and not having the foresight to see that two and a half centuries or so later an inept and stressed bloke from Gloucester would be trying to steer his new boat home through their canal system. One more thought; how many of the structures that we construct today will still be standing and functional in three hundred years' time?

Boaters often affectionately refer to the canal as the "Cut"; this was a term used when a canal was being constructed by "cutting" through the land. To start with I did not use the term because I thought that perhaps only time-served "real boaters" should use it; and I would have felt like an imposter if I had uttered the word.

At this time I still had not learnt the boat-handling skills that would make me a better boater and enable me to start enjoying myself; for now, I was having to concentrate so hard that it was making me fatigued. I was still over-correcting when attempting to steer and this was quite stressful, even more so when approaching the narrow parts of the canal and when boats were coming in the other direction. I'm sure that other boaters must have wondered what the hell I was doing as I made my drunken way along the Cut. I found holding the boat still in one place impossible and mooring the boat was also traumatic.

If I had to offer advice to a new boater it would be this: if when you first start your boating life on the canal or river you are unlucky enough to experience the same problems and emotions as me, stick with it, over time things WILL start to fall in to place you WILL start to relax and you WILL get better and start to enjoy your life on the water!

Due to my then lack of confidence, I was happy to let Dave do most of the steering but I had to reluctantly accept that this was not the way forward. Eventually we decided on taking it in turns to steer *Akita*, walk the dog, and make the tea, until we reached Kidderminster.

Upon arriving at Kidderminster, David; who considers himself a bit of a chef, insisted on making lunch of bacon and egg rolls. The eggs, having made a bid for freedom, must have jumped out of the frying pan only to perish in the flame of the gas hob because they were "very-well-done" (don't tell Dave I told you).

The canal runs right through the town and from where we had moored for Dave's "gourmet" lunch I could see a Halfords store within easy walking distance. It seemed prudent to get a new battery to start the engine, the last thing I wanted to do was to have it stall on the River Severn and have to go through the rigmarole of lifting the engine bay cover, connecting the booster battery, etc., while screaming like a baby and drifting out of control down-river and heading to a weir!

Now "easy walking distance" turns out to be relative, depending on whether you are carrying a heavy starter battery and trying to hold back an over-enthusiastic dog on a very hot day. A new battery was purchased and carried with ever-extending arms back to the *Akita* of the floating type, where Dave connected it to the battery leads.

We then decided to give it a test, but, on turning the key, nothing happened. I checked the connection and found a fault with the way the leads had been reconnected. Test number two produced the same results.

'Hang on, I've got it, the pull-cord safety cut-off link is not in place,' I said. 'OK, try it now,' STILL NOTHING! Then realisation dawned, the gear lever was not in the neutral position! Neutral was selected and while holding our breath (well, not Stanley who was panting like a stream train on this hot day in early May), we turned the key ... and the engine fired into life!

After another "relatively" short walk to a garage for fuel we were ready to cast off once more. With Dave at the helm and Stanley safely aboard we untied the mooring ropes and I pushed *Akita* out onto the Cut and walked the short distance to the next lock. A boater coming the other way shouted over to us that he had trouble getting through; and once we tried to exit the lock ourselves we could see what he had meant. I could not get the gate fully open to allow *Akita* to exit; Dave tried to clear any debris away from behind the lock gate with the boat hook but in the end I just had to lean as hard as I could on the gate balance beam (the leaver to push the gate open and closed) and Dave just managed to squeeze *Akita* through.

I had thought the locks would be a pain in the behind; but in fact I was now starting to enjoy operating them – we were starting to get a system going and were working our way through most with ease.

Here's the process:

I approach the lock, windlass and anti-vandal key in hand (the windlass is used to wind the paddles up and down to allow water in and out of the lock chamber, the anti-vandal key is sometimes needed to unlock the paddles). First I check if the lock is "set" correctly for us (either full or empty as required); if it is not set in our favour I make sure there is no boat coming the other way who can use the lock the way it is set, this saves water and in fact does not cost you any time as the lock will then be set correctly for you once the other boat leaves. If the lock is not set correctly I wind the paddles to let the water in/out, once the water level has equalised I push open the gates, close the paddles, and the boat is driven in. The gates are then closed and another set of paddles operated to readjust the water level, the opposite gates are opened, boat driven out, gates and paddles all closed and locked, then cruise on down the Cut, simple!

When controlling a boat in a lock you should try to avoid hitting the lock gates with the bow of your boat, but it is even more important to keep your stern well clear of the rear of the lock especially when "locking down". At the rear of the lock, hidden under the water there is a step or "cill" (sill); you should keep the stern clear (forward) of this, otherwise when the water level drops the rudder or stern of your boat can become hung up on the cill. The front edge of the cill is indicated in most locks by a sign or painted marks, so as long as you are aware of its existence you should be fine.

When I was steering *Akita* through the locks I enjoyed the change of view and atmosphere as the lock was filled or emptied. When "locking down" (emptying) the scenery is replaced by lock walls covered with green slime dripping water into the chamber, sunlight is replaced by the cool gloom in the lower recesses, and in some locks there were narrow elongated cracks in the walls and water would be streaming out of them. When I was locking down the first few times, it was difficult not to make the joke "I'm sinking" as the boat descended, but this wore thin after a while.

"Locking up" was a different experience; I would steer *Akita* into the narrow lock chamber; usually bumping into something on the way in, and then be dripped on from the slime above. Dave would close the gates, completing a "hemmed-in" feeling. The paddles would be operated to allow water to fill the chamber and *Akita* would emerge out of the lock into the sunlight like a submarine surfacing. I was worried how Stanley would cope in the claustrophobic recesses of the chamber and how he would react to the noise of the rushing water, but the brave boy took it all in his stride.

With new battery on board and lessons learnt on the

more subtle points of starting the engine and working the locks, we left the town of Kidderminster behind and cruised through some agreeable countryside south-west towards Stourport-on-Severn and our appointment with the mighty River Severn.

The Mighty River Severn

At two hundred and twenty miles long; the River Severn is the longest river in Britain; flowing from its source in the Welsh mountains to the sea at the Bristol Channel. The river is navigable from just north of Stourport for some forty-six miles to the city of Gloucester; at Gloucester boaters leave the river to continue their voyage south on the Gloucester & Sharpness Canal.

The current of the river can be dramatically affected by rainfall, making boating "exciting"; in addition the Severn is subject to spring tides as far north of Gloucester as the Upper Lode Lock near the town of Tewkesbury. Just to make things even more entertaining; the tidal parts of the Severn are also affected by the "Severn Bore"; a natural phenomenon which is basically a wave of varying size which travels back up the river at speeds of up to 13mph, (the largest wave recorded was around 9.2 foot (2.8 m).

When planning the cruise home the one thing that caused me more loss of sleep than anything else was the thought of going on the River Severn! I simply did not know what to expect. How fast would the water be flowing? Would the engine on the boat be powerful enough? Would I be able to steer the boat? In the event of the engine failing I would have to come up with a system to deploy the anchor, would it hold or how far would it drag before it bit and how would I get it back on board if we were lucky enough to get the engine going again?

Would there be a lot of big boats on the river and how would they know that I did not have a clue what I was doing?

As we approached Stourport it dawned on me that I was responsible for the boat and any consequences should we have an accident. I was starting to get nervous and as soon as we were through York Street Lock I moored *Akita* and checked the fuel level – the last thing I wanted to do was run out of fuel on the river! I strapped Stanley into his XXL-size doggy lifejacket, put on my coat, and donned my own bright red buoyancy aid. To give Dave credit he could see I was anxious and he offered to steer *Akita* on the first bit of the river, to which I readily agreed!

Stourport is basically made up of the Upper Basin, Clock Basin, and the Lower Basins. There are two separate sets of locks that lead to and from the river; these broad locks can accommodate craft with a beam of up to 16 foot and lead on to the river from the southern part of the Lower Basin. We were heading to the narrow locks and these can be found approximately 100 metres further north up the river from the broad locks.

I could tell Dave was apprehensive about navigating through the Stourport Basins for the first time. I went forward to the bow with a little radio to help by looking for the signs directing us towards the river; but I shouldn't have bothered, the signage was very good! Following the signs, we headed though the Upper Basin, turned right and into the Clock Basin, we then swung left towards the first of the narrow locks that would drop us down into the Lower Basin. After working the first of the locks I was getting warm and had stripped my buoyancy aid and coat off and deposited them back on the boat for Stanley to get his dog hair and slobber all over.

As I was starting to work the penultimate lock a small crowd of "Gongoozlers" (onlookers) had gathered so I tried my best to look like a salty sea dog for whom the river held no fear.

My apprehension grew as we worked our way through the last lock and as I closed the last lock gate and stepped back on board any pretence of Popeye-like seamanship was quickly dispelled as I shouted to Dave, with some degree of panic in my voice, 'DON'T GO FORWARD ON TO THE RIVER UNTIL I HAVE MY BUOYANCY AID ON!'

Dave sat at the wheel looking cool and waited for me to don my comfort blanket, whereupon he pushed the throttle forward, while I held on to Stanley, ready to swim to the bank after the capsize that must surely follow once we emerged into the current.

We cruised sedately onto the mighty River Severn and the lack of anything dramatic happening was a massive relief! We did not get swept downstream to be wrecked on a weir and did not get trampled under the bow of a big ship.

The Severn was very kind to us on our first day on the river and I felt a bit silly about my insistence on wearing my buoyancy aid after the total lack of any aquatic-related incident.

We only had to cruise for about a mile before reaching our mooring for the night, where we managed to tie up without incident to a pontoon at the Stourport Marina.

While Dave sorted out the boat I took Stanley to the marina grounds to give him a chance to add something to the contents of the river (he had been on the boat for a while and needed to "go"). We then walked over to the office to pay for our night's mooring, where I met Mal one of the marina's staff. He proved to be most amicable and very helpful to this new boater, offering solicited advice in abundance.

It was a beautiful spring afternoon so, with Stanley in full agreement, Dave and I decided to walk the half mile or so to Lincomb Lock. The lock would be the first of the manned large river locks that we would have to pass through on the way home. The river lock was to us yet another complete unknown and I was keen to have a look at one from dry land and if possible seek advice from the lock-keeper. The keeper could not have been more helpful and by the time we were walking back to the marina a lot of the mystery about river locks had been dispelled and we knew a lot more about what to expect. I was starting to notice that boat people are a friendly lot and always seem happy to offer advice or help out!

That evening the three of us walked back along the riverside to Stourport to seek nutrition in the form of our second curry of the trip; the route required that we walk back in the direction of the Stourport Basins. It was a nice feeling to amble around the basins and locks seeing the route we had taken in the boat and now felt acquainted with. The apprehension that we had felt about finding our way through the basins and on to the river had faded to be replaced with a quiet confidence and a pleasant familiarity.

Stanley and I waited on the path beside the noisy and very busy main road, watching the cars speeding past and over the bridge that traverses the River Severn. There were numerous people trying to cross the road and at one point a driver slowed to a stop to allow a family to cross; they did not acknowledge this small kindness and the fuming driver sped off over the bridge pouring smoke from his tyres and obscenities from his mouth. Stanley was not impressed and we were both pleased when Dave emerged from the curry house, white plastic bag of spicy food in hand, and we could leave the urban throng behind and return to the relative peace of the marina to eat.

Once we had devoured the curry, the tins, tubs, and the naan bread that Stanley had chewed, then left on the floor, were cleared away, we settled down once more to endure the storm of Stanley's nightly emissions. Dave shouted over to me from his bunk with desperation in his voice,

27

'You don't think that dog of yours is going to make that noise again tonight?' to which Stanley answered with a loud snore! Laughing; I replied, 'Does that answer your question?'

Southbound from Stourport

The following morning, after another night of a re-enactment of the blitz, a stupefied Dave emerged from his sleeping bag in search of breakfast. I had already eaten my customary four Weetabix topped with Rice Krispies, hot milk, and brown sugar.

The previous evening while searching for a curry house we had spotted a "Greasy Joes" type burger van just outside the marina, their notice board declared they would be serving breakfast rolls. Stanley needed a walk so the three of us set off together in search of morning sustenance for Dave.

We arrived just as the cook was walking across the yard back towards his burger van and at the same time as a rat ran out from under it.

I don't claim to be a mind reader but in this instance I knew exactly what everyone was thinking ...

Me: 'I'm glad I've already eaten!'

Dave: 'Shit, I can't walk away now; I'll just have to order food and hope it's OK.'

The cook: 'Shit, I hope they didn't see that rat'.

The rat: 'Look at the size of that dog; I hope he hasn't seen me!'

Stanley: 'Must chase that rat!'

Ratty: 'Oh shit!'

To save any embarrassment, the cook, Dave, and I all pretended that we had not seen the rat, but Stanley, who does not seem to suffer from any awkwardness, dispelled that illusion by trying to rip my arm out of its socket while he accelerated away in hot pursuit of Ratty. Ratty was now unavailable for any further comment!

Once the rat had made good his escape, we sat down at a wobbly table for Dave to eat his now-suspect breakfast roll alfresco, this gave me time to have a look around. A fascinating array of boats had been craned out of the water and as far as I could see most been left on dry land to die. Some, however, were being worked on and presumably others were lived in. I could have spent the whole day just walking around the "Boat Graveyard" looking at the assorted craft, but alas we were on a schedule and we had to move on.

One of the items that I had purchased via the internet was a handheld VHF marine radio – this would now prove to be a useful acquisition. All of the locks on the River Severn and some of the bridges on the Gloucester & Sharpness Canal have radios; they monitor on channel 74.

We cast off from the pontoon at Stourport Marina; I could have sworn that I could see the diminutive figure of Ratty waving us off with a tear in his eye as we headed once more onto the river. I knew from listening to the VHF radio that a large cruiser was heading downstream towards Lincomb Lock, the cruiser was still up-river behind us and not yet in sight. As we were approaching the lock I called the keeper on the radio and he instructed us to moor up before the lock to allow the bigger boat to go first.

Before we got to the lock, we would have to pass our first ever river weir. On the approach to the lock the river would split, we would have to make sure that we took the left-hand fork toward the lock and keep away from the right-hand side of the river which led to the weir. We would have to do this while keeping an eye out for oncoming traffic; this was one of the things that had kept this total novice awake at night with fears of being wrecked. In the event I did not have to worry – there's a boom across the right-hand fork to catch the unwitting boater, and we cruised down the correct fork and moored by the lock without incident.

Having the VHF radio was a real aid; it gave me an overview of what was going on around me and thus took a bit more of the mystery and stress away. I would recommend anyone planning to cruise the rivers and larger canals in the UK to get a VHF marine radio! However, be warned: before you use your radio you should take the RYA VHF Radio Course and be issued with a Certificate of Competence and Authority to Operate, this is a legal requirement!

The locks and bridges on the River Severn and Gloucester & Sharpness Canal operate a traffic-light system:

Red –STOP, do not enter the lock/pass the light or go through the bridge

Flashing Red – the Lock/Bridge-keeper has seen you, but you still need to stop.

Green – You may enter the lock/pass through the bridge.

The large cruiser appeared from up-river and had the green light so she cruised straight into the lock. Once the cruiser was held to the side by her ropes, the lock-keeper called *Akita* in. We cruised in and, as was now customary, bumped into the wall. Once in the lock, the bow line (rope) was passed through a steel cable that runs vertically from the bottom of the lock to the top – the same happens at the stern. These lines are held by hand, NOT tied off, and are simply used to hold the boat to the side of the lock wall and to stop it drifting around inside the chamber once the water level is altered. The ropes should be held tight enough to hold the boat in place but should be allowed to slip up and down the vertical cables as the boat ascends or descends. Once the ropes were in place the stressful part of the operation was over and all we had to do was hold on to the ropes. The large lock doors were closed by their hydraulics and the water level was lowered, and as it did so the craft in the lock descended too. Once the water level was equalised with that of the downstream river the gates were opened. We waited for the large cruiser to depart; then, after she had got well clear, we followed.

We now had four miles of river to travel before we would arrive at Holt Lock, the large cruiser was leaving us well behind in her wake and we had the river to ourselves; so for the first time since we had been on the river we were free to relax (sort of) and experiment. We tried slow turns and all was well, no water rushed over the gunwale and the boat did not flounder. Our confidence grew so we tried a 180-degree turn and headed back up stream against the current, again all was well! *Akita*'s little engine surged her forward against the powerful flow of the River Severn and we were making good time back up-river!

With ever-growing faith in our little boat, the bow was swung back around towards the south and we headed down-river to Holt Lock. As we approached; the lock was called up on the radio and we were given the green light allowing us to cruise straight in; like old hands we passed ropes through the cables and the lock keeper soon had us on our way.

After around three miles we passed the newly re-opened Droitwich Barge Canal and then shortly thereafter we arrived at Bevere lock. The lock was passed through cleanly and our confidence was soaring, three miles further on and we arrived in the city of Worcester, nicely in time for lunch.

No Worries at Worcester

Desperate to avoid another one of Dave's fried-up (cremated) masterpieces; I decided to find a mooring in the city and in turn edible food. To my pleasant surprise there were plenty of mooring places right in the centre of the city, In fact it was a lot easier to "Park" the boat than it would have been to find a place for a car! (Note: there is a fee to moor here and you can pay at the meter in the car parks next to the river). As all seasoned boaters know (and those of us who know it all in theory from lots of reading) when mooring on a river you should do so with your bow facing up-river into the current, so it was with confidence gained from our previous tentative practice we turned around, headed to the bank, and moored in a way that seemed to us to be like true professionals; we were starting to get the hang of this boating thing!

We had moored just down-river from Sabrina Footbridge and next to the Worcester Race-course. As we were getting Stanley out of the boat a large cruiser was attempting to moor in front us; the "Captain," obviously stressed was screaming and shouting at his crew, he was still shouting as we walked away when as far as we could see the boat was securely tied to its mooring.

The River Severn cuts through Worcester and the east bank is quite high, so we had to ascend on steps away from the waterway in the search of food. It was still a lovely sunny day; if a little windy but we did not have far to go before finding a café with some outside tables, this was ideal for a party with a large dog in tow. I secured a table and while Dave went in to order two extra-large all day breakfasts I had to answer the usual questions about Stanley:

'What is his name?'

'What sort of dog is he?'

'How much does he weigh?'

'How old is he?'

'How much does he eat?'

Then that are the typical comments:

'Oh isn't he beautiful!'

'He looks just like a bear!'

'I bet he eats a lot!'

'What a big dog!'

And my all-time personal favourite:

'Who takes who for a walk?' (I like to think it's me that dictates the walk!)

Once Dave had returned with our fodder we tucked in with relish, trying to eat the food before the wind could cool it too much. Stanley, for all his size, is very good at the table and knows that if he waits and does not make a fuss he will get a treat once the humans have finished eating. As is normal I saved the "Stanley bits" for him ready to show just how well I have trained and how well I can control this big dog that was currently lying on the floor at my feet. 'Sit,' I said and Stanley sat up. I put titbit of food on the ground while saying 'WAIT!' Stanley waited, 'OK take it!' He took the piece of meat. The other normal tricks; paw, lie down, sit up, and more waiting to be told to take the food were preformed successfully, I was on a roll and the audience were impressed with how well I could control the big beast! Show over and feeling smug about how well my talent of being an animal trainer had been appreciated by the now extended crowd I stood up and was promptly and humiliatingly dragged over the grass toward the bushes for a wee. As mentioned before; unlike me, Stanley has no sense of embarrassment. OK, if the truth is told perhaps it is Stanley who takes me for a walk after all.

Dave made his way back to the *Akita* while Stanley (yep, you guessed), took me for a walk to work off some of his energy, this was important as we would be spending some time on the boat before arriving at our next destination and mooring for the night at Upton-upon-Severn.

Stanley and I made our way back to the river and walked alongside the large cruiser with the now mute captain and a crew that looked suitably chastised; (I thought boating was supposed to be fun!). We continued past the happy ship, and Stanley leapt on board *Akita*. Dave took the wheel; I cast off, and we came about to once again head down-river. The banks were full of people walking and lying on the grass; anglers were fishing from the paths alongside the river, and ducks and masses of swans were on the banks and swimming in the water. This part of the river as it heads through the city of Worcester is quite busy; boats of all sorts were on the Severn. An array of private cruisers were making their way straight through Worcester, while rowing boats bobbed about and other larger boats were taking fee-paying passengers on pleasure cruises up and down the river. The amount of river traffic had concerned me the first-time boater; but I should not have worried, we stuck to the "rules of the road" and kept a good lookout, and all was well.

I felt privileged to be able to see the views from a perspective that a non-boater would never see nor appreciate, it was an odd feeling to be sat on the foredeck of the boat well away from the sound of the engine, hearing the water breaking on the bow and watching the ever-changing scenery. What was that odd feeling? Well, I was starting to relax and enjoy myself; I was away from work, the sun was shining, I was on my very own boat with a good mate and my dog; this is what it was all about, this was what I was looking for! The only thing missing was poor Cat who was still at home convalescing; I thought had better take some photos for her!

When up and about Cat seems to spend most of her time looking at the world through the lens of a camera, she loves taking photos, which I sometime find annoying! I will be walking along with Cat by my side, then after a minute or so I will look around and she will be miles behind having stopped to take yet another snap, and it takes us an age to get anywhere! I guess I should not complain too much; sometimes the results are very good and as I usually have my hands full with Stanley I don't get (or even remember) to take many pictures, if Cat did not take them we would have very few to show for our efforts!

Photos taken, we continued to cruise southwards, quickly arriving at Diglis Lock, which is just down-river from Worcester. It is a double lock with the two chambers set side by side – the narrower one is set to the east side. I was not surprised when we were directed into this one, which was on our left as we cruised towards it. With yet another lock under our belts, we now had a clear run to our objective, the mooring for the night at Upton.

Cool Leather Hat

As a novice I did not want to spend a night moored on the flow of the river itself, so I had booked *Akita* into a mooring in Upton Marina. Not having been on the river before I did not know what the entrance to the marina would look like or when we would be approaching it, so I was using the bridge at Upton-upon-Severn as a landmark; the marina would be on the east bank to our left about a quarter of a mile past the bridge.

I was at the helm when we were approaching Upton Bridge so I started to look ahead for the entrance to the marina, as I looked forward I could see what looked to me like a VERY large boat coming the other way; it was a large leisure cruiser carrying fee-paying customers. This was no problem, I told myself, just keep to the right, follow the rules, and all will be well, but then to my horror the large vessel did not follow the script and it turned across the river onto "my side" and started to head towards little old me! I did not have a clue what she was doing, all I could do was throw *Akita* into reverse and panic! This was not a great feeling and this new boater felt completely out of his depth! Then to my relief it dawned on me what she was intending, she was going to the mooring on the west bank and was not planning to crush me under her bows. I was surprised how rapidly the situation could change from me getting ready to jump overboard with Stanley to swim for it (leaving Dave on board to finish making the tea), to just continuing to cruise down the river as if nothing had happened.

We glided under the bridge and past several boats tied up at Upton – too many in fact for the available moorings – so they were moored breasted-up (side by side) stretching out into the river three- or four-deep. We continued by the now safely tied up large passenger cruiser and on towards the marina. We passed the entrance, turned around, and, heading into the current, turned into Upton Marina. After some confusion as to where we were meant to tie up for the night we found our spot and switched the engine off.

It was a Saturday afternoon; and the Upton Folk Festival was still in full swing. We walked over the bridge that we had just sailed under and into the small town, looking for a shop to replenish our dwindling supply of milk. We decided to have a walk around the festival; all the pubs were open and it looked like they had been so all day, plenty of people singing old folk songs, pint glass in hand, and others were swaying along happily. There were quite a few stalls selling the usual hippy paraphernalia associated with this type of event. One stall did, however, grab our attention, it was selling amongst other things what I thought were cool-looking leather hats. Dave took an interest in them and after trying to haggle for a better price decided to walk away and think about it. We made our way through the crowd of people, getting stopped every other minute for people to admire and pat Stanley and to answer the predictable question of: "who takes who for a walk?"

As we emerged on to a quieter back street; I saw a sight that you don't see that often: another Akita! Of course Stanley and I had to go and say hello and I found myself in the odd position of asking the usual questions about name, age, weight, etc.; at least I did not ask the one about who takes who for a walk.

We found we had gone full circle and had arrived back at the hat stall, and ten minutes later, having paid the full asking price I was the proud owner of a cool-looking leather hat, justifying the expense by telling myself I would need it to keep the sun off when I was on the bridge of the boat!

We returned to the boat having spent a lot more than just the price of a few pints of milk, however, the good news was that we had managed to acquire a menu from the local curry house and they took orders by telephone!

Another good curry was consumed and after making use of the marina shower facilities we settled down to listen to Stanley mimicking anti-aircraft fire for the rest of the night, he was very good ...

Upton to Gloucester – Don't Hold Your Breath!

The following morning we were up nice and early, if somewhat red-eyed, ready to greet some "fresh blood" who would be joining our happy but sleep-deprived crew. My mum had driven her partner Noel, and another friend of mine, John, to Upton Marina so that they could cruise the last part of the River Severn to Gloucester aboard *Akita*. Stanley; who had slept very well was very pleased and excited to see them all. Dave H. was just happy to have someone to talk to about his insomnia and receive some well-deserved sympathy.

The closing times of the locks on the Severn vary throughout the year, but they normally start operating from 08.00. I wanted to time our arrival at Upper Lode Lock for just after it opened; this meant an early start. To avoid disturbing anyone sleeping aboard their boats (chance would be a fine thing), we cruised out of the marina as quietly as possible, waving to my mum as we went. I did look, but given the early hour none of Ratty's friends had turned out to bid us farewell.

Just over two miles later the first brew of the day was served and we passed under the high structure of the M50 bridge; it is of a utilitarian design but I was still fascinated as I studied it. The thing I noticed most was what I assumed were drainage ducts, it was another fine dry day, but had it been raining I could imagine water pouring from them straight into the river and wondered what the effect would be on someone standing on the exposed deck of a boat. Perhaps they were not drainage ducts but I like to think they were; I made a note to come back one rainy day. As we left the bridge and the would-be drainage ducts behind, I was struck once again by the unique view of objects afforded to people in boats.

Yet more tea was brewed and drunk and with Noel taking a turn at the wheel we headed south towards Tewkesbury. Here, on the east bank to our left, the navigable part of the River Avon added its contents into our river as we cruised around a right-hand bend. Shortly afterwards we arrived at the large Upper Lode Lock.

Leaving the lock astern, the terrain started to look familiar, if skewed from a boater's perspective. Some river-side pubs I frequented a decade or three ago while going through my "biker stage" were passed; I never guessed that years later I would be cruising past the same river-side pubs on a boat and not a motorcycle!

When planning the trip home I had made navigation notes; there were more notes for the next section of the Severn than for the whole of the trip so far:

Haw Bridge – KEEP to the west side (right when going downstream) when going under the bridge! (Apparently there is a submerged obstruction near to the east bank.)

Wainlode Hill – KEEP to the north side (right when going downstream) You will see signs directing you to keep right!

And now as the river continued to meander south we would soon be reaching the "Upper Parting".

The name "Upper Parting" describes itself, it is where the River Severn splits or "parts" just over two miles north of Gloucester Lock, the river then rejoins at the predictably named "Lower Parting", thus creating Alney Island. Alney Island is a great place to walk your dog; but is a nature reserve so keep an eye on your dog and don't let it disturb the wildlife!

The west channel is no longer navigable, so all river traffic must take the east channel toward Gloucester Lock then leave the river to continue south on the Gloucester & Sharpness Ship Canal.

South of the Upper Parting the navigable east channel of the Severn narrows dramatically and twists and turns with some blind corners thrown in for good measure. The River Severn is used by commercial vessels and these tend to be large, it would not be fun to unexpectedly meet one of these coming the other way when on this constricted part of the river!

My notes for this section of the trip read as follows:

Upper Parting:

1-   TAKE the EAST channel (left when going down stream).

2-   Send a LOOKOUT forward! – Watch out for large tree in river 200m north of Westgate Bridge (should be marked with buoys). Also look out for oncoming vessels!

3-   Call Gloucester Lock to check if any large vessels are heading north towards you and to have the lock made ready. Gloucester Lock MUST GET THERE BEFORE 17.45! Once you have a green light to enter the lock KEEP CLOSE TO THE WALL ON THE LEFT as you approach the lock!

We arrived at the Upper Parting and dry-mouthed I pressed the push to talk button on my little hand-held VHF radio and spoke into the microphone, 'Hello, Gloucester Lock from *Akita*, over,' to my surprise the lock-keeper responded assuring me that only one narrowboat was heading up-river and no other large vessels were northbound towards me, he would also have the lock ready for me to cruise straight in (great service).

We took the east channel and sure enough the river narrowed significantly; after the wide expanse of the river to our north I now felt hemmed in by the tree-lined bank. Keeping a careful lookout ahead for the inbound narrowboat and fallen tree I steered *Akita* toward Gloucester.

The fallen tree was on the right side, lying well out towards the centre of the navigation, and river debris had collected all around it; however, I did not have time to absorb what flotsam and jetsam had been collected by its bulk. We had been on the river for a few hours and had not seen another boat and now, as luck would have it, on the most constricted part of the Severn we had come upon the fallen tree and the narrowboat at the same time, what joy I felt! Although I was heading downstream the narrowboat was closer to the obstruction, so making a snap decision I slowed *Akita* right down, trusting the other vessel would clear the obstacle before I needed to turn toward the other side of the river. We were still closing too fast so I engaged reverse, hoping our stern would not swing across the river in front of the oncoming boat. As I held my breath the very, very long narrowboat slowly, so slowly, cruised past on our port side. I tried to look relaxed and cool (I assumed my new hat would enhance my coolness) but I am sure the crew on the other boat was wondering why I was turning blue as I did my best to give them a cheery wave while trying not to pass out!

The two boats' sterns parted company, allowing me to breathe once more. I engaged forward gear while swinging the helm over to port, and ironically *Akita*'s bows missed the tree by a mile. Still trying to look nonchalant (I'm sure the hat was helping), while desperately trying to re-oxygenate my blood stream, I steered *Akita* along the snaking river towards our appointment with Gloucester Lock.

As you approach the lock there is a high wall on your port side, lengths of chains are attached along the extent of the wall, drooping down like bunting towards the powerful flow of the water. These chains are only used by boats to moor up to (stern first) in the event that they have to wait

43

for the lock. Due to the little VHF radio and the efficiency of the lock-keeper we did not require the chains or the stress that would have undoubtedly ensued.

My mum; having driven back down from Upton-upon-Severn a lot faster than we had cruised, stood on top of the wall to greet the intrepid sailors as we glided towards the lock.

The green light was reassuringly displayed, and as advised we cruised keeping our port side close to the wall so that we did not get pulled around the bend in the river past the lock to wreck on the weir that lies in wait just downstream. At the last moment, I steered *Akita* away from the wall and safely into the port side of Gloucester Lock and forward of the bridge that goes across the tail of the lock (the end nearest to the river).

Gloucester Lock was originally two locks in a staircase but now is just one elongated chamber; the recesses where the middle gates were located can still be seen. So far all the river locks had lowered us down to the height of the river below, at Gloucester Lock you "lock-up" to the level of the Gloucester Docks Basin and the Gloucester & Sharpness Canal some 16 foot above. The ascent can be turbulent and seemed to take an age but we were all happy as we had made good time on the river; the lock-keeper was predictably very helpful and, once the chamber was eventually full, an alarm was sounded and the gates with the footbridge attached were swung open allowing me to take our craft into Gloucester Docks for the first time.

The Docks and the Gloucester & Sharpness Canal

Work first started on the Gloucester & Sharpness Canal (G&S) in 1794 and continued for a few years until funds ran out; by this time over five miles of canal had been cut. It was well over a decade before work continued and the ship canal was finally opened in 1827 – at the time it was the widest and deepest canal in the world.

The canal was built to bypass the treacherous and now largely unnavigable part of the River Severn; vessels heading up-river from the Bristol Channel and wishing to continue north past the city of Gloucester must leave the river sixteen and a half miles south of Gloucester at Sharpness, here they take the G&S to Gloucester Docks where they can then lock back down onto the river to continue north. Likewise boats heading south on the river must lock up at Gloucester and then take the canal south towards Sharpness.

The Gloucester & Sharpness Canal is fed with water via streams running down from the Cotswolds. To supplement this supply, and to replace water that is lost due to evaporation, extraction, and when the locks are operated, more water is needed. This water is pumped up from the River Seven and into Gloucester docks – this keeps the basin and canal at the correct level. New pumps were installed around 2001. The old pump (which looks remarkably like a snail) can now be seen displayed on the West Quay near to the dry docks.

Gloucester Docks is also home to the Gloucester

Waterway Museum; which is housed in the Llanthony Warehouse, a grade two listed building right on the dockside. There are displays on most aspects on canal life, construction, and wildlife; there are several boats that are part of the museum fleet and these are moored right outside. The fleet include two "trip boats" the *Queen Boadicea II* and the *King Arthur* (more on the *Queen Boadicea II* later). There are also old working narrowboats; you can step onboard to get a feel of what it must have been like living aboard in the cramped conditions of the small rear cabin of these vessels. In addition there is an old steam dredger and a barge.

A Bridge too Far

I have been to Gloucester many times over the years but never aboard a boat – it evoked an odd feeling to be on the water in my own craft in a place I knew so well. The first thing I realised was that I did not know the place at all! That may seem strange but walking around the docks as a non-boater your perspective is completely different, for instance you are not interested in where the water points, refuse, or Elsan disposal points are or where the moorings are located. As the wind had picked up, causing me to drift around the busy docks I indeed did have an acute interest in finding a place to moor!

I headed over to a pontoon in the north-east corner of the main basin, not really sure if I was allowed to stop there, and attempted to moor without crashing into other boats. *Akita* was tied up without a collision and we all stepped ashore (well, onto a floating pontoon). John and Noel were leaving us here while Dave, Stanley, and I would continue along the G&S to our new home mooring at Saul Marina.

We had made good time to Gloucester, so Stanley decided that he would take us for a walk for a much-needed wee and that while we were at it we should go and see his other "Uncle Dave" (another friend of mine called Dave B.). We walked along the pontoon towards the lock. The lock gates were now closed, allowing us to use the footbridge affixed to them and we walked past "Lock Warehouse" and over a wooden-arched footbridge which spanned the part of the River Severn that leads to the weir, and then stepped onto Alney Island.

Feeding the ducks at Saul Marina

Stanley loved the freedom that the long-line retractable lead afforded him and made full use of the length to maximise the opportunity to sniff, run about, then indulge in a movement that required I clean up after him then deposit my "trophy" in one of the many receptacles that are provided in the area. (I told you the island was a good place to walk your dog.)

We walked north alongside the river, following it back upstream, crossed over yet another footbridge, and met up with "Uncle Dave B." outside his place of work. After relating the story of our adventure so far we left Dave B. to his labour and made our way back to *Akita*, this time taking the more direct route past Gloucester Prison.

After a discussion about whether we should get a pizza or not (I wanted the pizza) David decided that he would prepare food for us, this time in the form of a ham, cheese, and pickle sandwich while I chauffeured us south along the G&S. Lamenting the missed opportunity of devouring a pepperoni-topped stone-baked pizza; and dreading what food was to be served, I swung *Akita* around and left Gloucester Docks, passing underneath Llanthony bascule bridge, which the keeper kindly raised for us. Opening this bridge required that the pedestrians and some road traffic be stopped, and it was an odd feeling to have this large bridge opened just for us.

David appeared from the galley; supper-sized club sandwich presented proudly on a plate and offered me the results of his culinary endeavour, dubiously I took it from him and after a pause to fortify my resolve and to give my taste buds fair warning I chomped into it ... Dave was right he really can cook!

While Stanley eyed my "supper sandwich" with relish (that's looking at it with relish, there was no relish on the sandwich), Hempsted Bridge was swung aside for us to pass and with a wave to thank the efficient keeper, and while trying to avoid the rowers who were practising on the canal, we continued on down the G&S for the first time.

A green light was showing on the approach to Sims Bridge so we cruised under the bridge, which has an air draft of three metres.

I was amazed by the number of anglers who were sitting on the bank, their long rods extending out towards the middle of the wide ship canal. The fishermen (yes they were all men) were spaced evenly along the towpath like an army ready to do battle with some unseen underwater threat. I imagined how proud their wives must feel that their husbands were not with them safe at home, but were here on a sunny Sunday afternoon to protect us all from this hidden aquatic menace (perhaps I should fit *Akita* with depth charges). Alternatively perhaps the valiant hunters' spouses were just happy to get them out of the house.

Seeing the amount of gear that this legion of brave hunters of the deep had with them to help combat the

49

threat from below, I could see that they took their mission very seriously and decided to give them a wide berth in case I got caught in the crossfire.

On the approach to Rea Bridge we also were shown a green light; great, we thought, under we go, however, as we got closer to the still-closed bridge I was beginning to have misgivings. To me the bridge looked too low for *Akita* to pass under safely with her stern deck roof still up. I slowed down but the bridge-keeper, now lying on the floor to better assess the clearance, beckoned me on with some enthusiasm and his face exhibiting confidence. My suspicions allayed, I pushed the throttle forward and the engine surged us onward. As *Akita*'s bow and then cabin roof passed under the bridge it became obvious to me that the roof over my head was not going to make it, this thought was reflected in the face of the bridge-keeper which was now no longer "exhibiting confidence", in fact it was showing just the opposite! I slammed *Akita*'s gear box into reverse and watch helplessly as her momentum drew my soon to be ex-roof towards the steelwork of the bridge.

The propeller bit into the water and finally our boat slowed and stopped with inches to spare and we slowly backed away from the bridge. I shouted over to the bridge-keeper, telling him I would lower the roof, but, ever-helpful, the keeper would not hear of it, and simply swung the bridge open for us. With a wave to the now-smiling keeper and the audience that had stopped on the towpath to watch the show, roof still intact, we chugged on down the wide canal.

So far we had been lucky (very lucky at Rea Bridge) in the fact that we had green lights all the way. However, as we approached Parkend Bridge our luck was to desert us. Dave was steering, we were over on the wrong side of the channel in an effort to avoid becoming collateral damage in the ongoing battle between the fish and gentlemen on the embankment, and we were shown a red light. Being total novices we approached the light in the misguided assumption that it would change for us, but the light remained resolutely red!

Unnoticed by us, the wind speed had picked up; it had little or no effect on the handling of the boat while we were cruising at a steady pace, however, as we were now rapidly approaching the still-red light we were left with little choice other than to slow to a virtual stop. The lack of much forward momentum had a dramatic effect on our narrow draft, lightweight boat. With the wind pushing us we began to drift further over the canal into the path of an oncoming craft, both Dave and I paralysed and because of our lack of experience were powerless to react. We were getting some bemused looks from the rightly irritated crew on the oncoming vessel. By this time we had drifted past the traffic light and I was hanging over the back of the boat in an attempt to keep it in sight. Just as I was about to lose visual contact with the light, it at long last changed to a wonderful shade of green. Another lesson learnt; lesson being that when you see a red light slow right down to give yourself plenty of room between you and the light and if it is windy keep some forward momentum so you can keep control of the boat. We still had so much to learn!

It was just over a mile to the final bridge of our epic cruise; but that was not long enough for us to settle down after our near miss, or to come to terms with the fact that we were going to struggle to control the boat in the increasing wind at the very slow speeds that would be required to negotiate the turns into the marina.

And so it was that two stressed and nervous new boaters, with a new-found healthy respect for and a slight fear of the strengthening wind, approached the bridge at Saul Junction. What was to follow was not the best way to introduce *Akita* or her fledgling crew to the population of the Saul Junction area.

Making an Entrance

Saul Junction is laid out as follows: cruising south you pass Junction Bridge and immediately after the bridge to the east (left) is the entrance to the Stroud Water Canal, continuing south and straight after the bridge is a turning basin. Junction Bridge is a footbridge that is swung aside by the keeper as boats approach, situated in a very pretty location with a white bridge-keeper's cottage next to it and plenty of grass for onlookers to sit and watch the comings and goings of boats at this very busy junction. None of this was noticed by us, the two new boaters with a lot on our minds and any confidence gained on the trip thus far evaporating in the wind, nor did we notice the large sign stating NO LEFT TURN!

With Dave still at the wheel we drifted passed Junction Bridge at a snail's pace and, watched by the crowd residing on the freshly clipped grass, attempted to turn left into the Stroud Water Canal. Due to the wind, acute angle of the turn, the fact that you are not meant to turn left in the first place, coupled with our total lack of boat-handling ability, we never had a chance and simply crashed in slow-motion into the wall. After another attempt, and another impact, common sense prevailed and we proceeded into the basin, sheepishly turned around and headed toward the turn from the correct direction, then promptly crashed into the side again. After yet another attempt, and being lucky not to lose any fenders, we scraped our way through the narrow entrance and onto the Stroud Water Canal. A short distance later and with the same degree of skill (or lack thereof) we turned right in to *Akita*'s new home, Saul Marina, and introduced ourselves to our new neighbours in the worst way possible.

By this time our nerves were as splintered as the wooden guard rails running down the side of the hull and we still had the worst bit to go, mooring *Akita* into the very narrow gap between the pontoon and the 30-foot cruiser belonging to Mark, our soon-to-be neighbour.

Dave H. sat at the helm scrutinising the small gap, not looking happy at all! Hoping that he would say 'No I'm fine', I offered to take *Akita* into her mooring but Dave jumped out of the seat saying, 'You take her in; I don't want to be responsible for any damage to other boats!' I could not blame Dave for this, so with heavy heart I sat at the wheel and proceeded to be carried by the wind in every direction other than into our mooring. At one point we made it to our pontoon; Dave stepped onto it with rope in hand but then *Akita* was blown across the marina and was T-boned crosswise along another pontoon containing longer narrowboats, leaving Dave standing there watching helplessly.

I was on my own on the boat with only Stanley to offer any advice. I was stressed, nervous, embarrassed, had no control over the boat, and was wishing we had never bought it!

After more attempts than I can remember, lots of sweat, shouting, cursing, and help from other boaters *Akita* was dragged kicking, screaming, and scrapping into her mooring with more than a little bump into Mark's boat. (As I have been told many times since: "Boating is a contact sport.") I stepped out of *Akita* with wobbly legs and if I was given to dramatics I would have kissed the pontoon. Stanley jumped out of the boat and ran to the nearest bush for a wee, so he must have been nervous too! Boat secured; and with tails between our legs we quickly left the marina for the short drive home.

Hi Honey, We're Home – Time to Start Work!

Both Stanley and I were very happy to see Cat after being away for three nights. Cat was still convalescing and had not seen our new boat, we had planned for her to spend a quiet day at the marina the following day, which was a bank holiday Monday. However, as it was still early evening and the sun was shining we decided to leave Stanley at home for a well-earned rest while Cat and I drove to the marina for her first look at our new vessel. On the drive down I was at pains to point out to her that she should see the potential in the boat, and not the current state of the interior, made worse by the fact that two blokes and a large dog had been living on it, surviving mainly on curry and mugs of tea.

Due to her silence I was not sure how Cat felt on seeing *Akita* for the first time, but I wished I had made an attempt to tidy up a bit before we had abandoned ship earlier in the day!

The next day work started in earnest; the mess left on board was soon buried under a mountain of tools and equipment as *Akita*'s cabin started to resemble a building site. Not having any running water was the biggest pain on our trip home so this was first on the list. There was no way the main tank or existing plumbing could be brought back online any time soon so two large jerrycans, a 12-volt submersible water pump, tap, and some piping were installed, and, hey presto we had running water.

There is an electric hook up at the marina; so to make

the work on *Akita* more efficient a 240-volt distribution board, mains sockets, and lights were next on the agenda. This was a straightforward job and took no time at all. Next came the bed.

We both wanted a big comfortable bed, as we did not want to feel like we were roughing it like campers. I had no idea to start with, but it soon became apparent that building a bespoke bed from scratch would be one of the single most expensive projects on the boat. The price of wood is astonishing and a large double bed takes a lot of wood! Then there is the price of good-quality foam to make the mattresses, also shocking! After measuring, sawing, drilling, countersinking, and fixing, the bed frame was finally assembled. Once the bed was constructed; we had two comfortable bench seats along each side of the boat with loads of storage underneath them; these can be used as two single beds, allowing you to walk through the centre, or, as we prefer, can be made into one king-size double bed. The bed may have been eye-wateringly expensive, but I now have somewhere to lie down to recover from the shock and it was well worth the cost and exertion!

We now had a perfect space at the end of the bed opposite the gas cooker to build an open-fronted cabinet with a counter top (you can never have too much counter space). This unit was built by the ever-helpful Noel, and is used for a small 240-volt cooker/hob, a microwave, and an electric kettle. There is a handy space at the bottom for a bin. A small table originally removed from our camper van was mounted in the dining area.

To stop Stanley slipping all over the place, and to help with insulation; the poorly laid laminate floor was covered with gym matting, this also helps reduce the clatter of Stanley's claws!

The floral curtains were replaced by white blinds; these looked great from the outside and helped modernise the look of the boat.

Next on the ever-expanding list was the 12-volt system; a split charger controller and new leisure battery were acquired along with a solar panel. Loads of interior lights were installed along with sockets to power radios and charge mobile phones and laptops, etc. The bilge pump to take the water away from the shower tray was reconnected and a new bilge pump was also installed just in case we ever took on water. The tunnel lights and horn were rewired and navigation lights installed.

Rod, a very experienced boater, is our other marina neighbour whose boat I don't hit every time I return to the marina, but only because there is a pontoon in the way. Rod was busy painting the roof of his own boat but he took time out to help me replace the broken ship-type steering wheel with a new one, and I fitted this with a steering knob, this made steering so much easier – I couldn't believe the difference it made!

Cat, now on the road to recovery, started to paint over the nasty green with white and cream to brighten the place up. This also had the effect of making the cabin lighter when the lights were on at night!

I even mounted a whip aerial with a spring at the base on the front of the cabin roof; this was cut to a length to be just higher that of the rear deck roof, so if it hit a low bridge we would know the stern deck roof was not going to make it underneath. A small streamer was tied to the top of the aerial to give us an idea of what the wind was doing.

During the work we had a fair amount of rain; this enabled me to find some of the leaks that were inevitably going to occur on a boat that has not been maintained. There were small leaks from two of the screws holding the roof handrail in place and a torrent of water came in through the front windows (luckily the new bed mattresses were not in place so did not get soaked). All leaks were easily stemmed and after about two months working every evening and weekends we had what we were aiming for, a nice comfortable little floating home from home.

There was still a lot to do; the shower and gas boiler were still off-line but we could do without them for now, the main thing was that we were happy and getting happier with *Akita* – the more time we spent on board, the more we liked her.

So now we had a boat we could comfortably live on for trips away, it was time to put it to the test, get out there and start to enjoy it, so we started to plan some little trips.

Open All Hours?

Unlike most of the canal network; the Gloucester & Sharpness Canal and the River Severn have all of their bridges and locks manned. This is great when the keepers are there, however, they are only open during specific times and these times change throughout the year. This severely limits your ability to cruise freely and get the most from the expensive river and canal licence!

As a result of this before you plan any trips the first thing you have to consider are the opening times. For instance, it takes around two hours of cruising from Saul Junction to get to Gloucester Lock. If you want to get a full-day cruise on the River Severn you will need to be at Gloucester Lock first thing in the morning, however, there are no early starts to enable you to get to the lock as soon as it opens because the bridges are all closed! So the answer is to cruise your boat up the evening before and leave it in Gloucester Docks, but if you are working during the day this is not always possible. Even in the summer the bridges close at the ridiculously early time of 19.00; so if you want to go for a summer evening cruise you simply cannot! If that was not bad enough, the opening times are even further reduced in the winter period, in fact the G&S is closed to pleasure craft on Tuesdays and Wednesdays and you have to give twenty-four hours notice to use the river locks at all throughout the winter period. So if you reside on the G&S and are employed you have to plan well!

The Gloucester Tall Ships Festival takes place at the docks; this is a large well-attended event. Five "tall ships" (large old-fashioned sailing ships) were going to be in the docks; water-based events were to take place in the basin, and there would be a multitude of stalls. Numerous bars and bands were going to be playing, even "Captain Jack Sparrow" of *Pirates of the Caribbean* fame was to make an appearance. Cat thought this would be a good first trip for her in *Akita*. Having left it a bit late we were lucky to book one of the last moorings that were available right in the docks itself.

Due to a combination of restrictions imposed because of the movement of the tall ships, the usual limited bridge-opening times, and the unfortunate fact that I have to work for a living, planning for what should have been a simple excursion swung into action. It turned out that the only way we could get *Akita* there within the constrained timeframe was to take a Thursday afternoon off work.

Plans made, mooring booked, and half-day holiday organised; all that was left to do was wait for the misery of the working week to slowly dissipate. Thursday morning finally elapsed and I was free to go home and then make my way to the boat.

Uncle Dave B. arrived at the house and after saying hello to Stanley and bye to Cat (she was going to join *Akita* at the docks on the Saturday) we jumped into the campervan for the drive to the marina to collect *Akita*. This Uncle Dave had not been on the boat before so I did my prepared safety brief and gave Dave some "expert" tuition on boating. Now the newly "trained" crew were ready to cast off and make our way north.

I managed to leave the marina, turn around in the basin, and cruise up to Gloucester without incident; I felt I was slowly getting better! We moored at a dilapidated floating mooring alongside a garage and, grabbing the removable fuel tank, I made my way over to the pumps to fill up. I had some odd looks from people in and around the garage when as far as they were concerned I appeared from nowhere clutching a "funny-looking jerrycan" heading towards the pumps. In truth it did feel a bit odd to be mooring a boat by a petrol station primarily used by road-going motor vehicles. Fuelled-up, we slipped our mooring ropes and continued towards Gloucester Docks.

Other boaters must have had the same problems with their timings getting into the docks for the weekend, because we ended up in a convoy of assorted boats all heading to their moorings. As we neared and then entered the docks basin, the convoy morphed into congestion, trying to be polite I waited my turn while a large Dutch barge attempted to turn around and then reverse into her mooring. After a while I started to drift in the increasing wind; not wanting a repeat of my attempt to get into my home mooring for the first time, I pushed the throttle forward. I had done my research and I knew where my reserved mooring was so I made the decision to move straight on to it. As I approached the berth I could see a fellow boater standing on the pontoon boathook in hand ready to assist boats into place in the ever-strengthening wind. As soon as *Akita* was within range he hooked on and pulled us safely into dock – good bloke! With *Akita* swaying in the strong wind but safely tied up, I headed home to get some sleep ready for another insufferable day in the office.

Tall Ships and New Toys

Friday evening arrived and Cat gave Stanley and me a lift to the docks. The plan was for man and dog to stay on the boat for the Friday night and the "Cat" would join us on Saturday morning.

We were moored right outside Fosters – a busy dockside pub; they had outside seating so sleep was not easily achieved until the merrymakers had quaffed the last of their pints and moved on to a nightclub, home to bed, or, if they had been lucky, someone else's bed. I was very happy with *Akita*'s newly constructed bunk and Stanley was content with the gym matting on the floor. We both settled down for our first night on our newly refurbished boat.

The following morning we were rudely awakened by the countless blaring seagulls that reside around Gloucester Docks. Stanley was taken for a walk on the very handy Alney Island and breakfast was had before settling down to wait for Cat to arrive and the day's proceedings to commence.

Cat was due to catch the bus into town then take a short walk to the docks; but ever the lady she was chauffeured directly to the docks in a taxi (such decadence). Now for the first time she was to board *Akita* for pleasurable purposes rather than to paint.

The strong wind of the previous few days had subsided and it was turning out to be a beautiful sunny day; even the ubiquitous seagulls seemed to have departed. We had "front row seats" on the rear deck of *Akita* to view the show taking place on the water in the main basin of Gloucester Docks. We saw "Vikings" kidnapping a lady of Gloucester and attempting to escape in their wooden longboat only to sail past the stern of *Akita* and crash into our neighbours' (thankfully) steel-hulled narrowboat. After apologising in perfect English to Gary who owned the narrowboat, the Vikings backed away from the modern marvel that they had collided with only to be quickly caught and dispatched by the "brave men of Gloucester" and the lady returned to dry land. The show was to be repeated thrice daily; although much to Gary's relief the crash into his boat was not on the program. For my part I was happy to note that I am not the only one on the waterways who crashes into things!

We saw the Blue Launch (a replica of a cutter from the time of Nelson) with "Royal Marines" firing several broadsides with their muskets. This was very loud and poor Stanley did not like it at all and was shaking by the time they had finished their show, which, unfortunately for Stanley, was also repeated several times a day.

There were even some guys, looking somewhat lost in the large docks, paddling about in the basin who had followed the River Severn from its source in the Welsh mountains to Gloucester and then onto Sharpness on the canal by first walking and then paddling standing up on boards.

We had been told by the landlady of Fosters pub that Stanley was allowed in to her establishment, so after meeting up with friends and family we all sat down to a good meal. Stanley as ever was well behaved and got his treats as reward.

As is the norm, Stanley was getting lots of attention with the stock questions being asked and answered, and lots of patting of his poor head took place. Stanley took all this in his stride but I did wonder if for all the activities and the attention, Stanley wouldn't rather be in a field somewhere trying to roll in fox poo?

During one of our walks around the docks we stopped to look through the door of a shop; to our surprise we were invited in with Stanley still in tow! Stanley likes going to shops (he's always trying to drag me in to them) so on this occasion he was very happy to actually be allowed in. Situated in the Upstairs Downstairs Antiques Emporium on Severn Road you will find R&B Canal Art. R&B also has a small chandlery (shop selling boating equipment) and there, leant up against the shelving, was a telescopic boathook that would float if you dropped in to the Cut; I had to have it, it was telescopic and it floated!

As the afternoon lapsed into evening, it was once again time to seek out some food, Stanley and I had been in and around the boat for almost twenty-four hours and so far not a single curry had been consumed. In my opinion this was a situation that was far from acceptable and needed to be rectified.

As you would expect of a once-working docks, Gloucester Docks Basin is surrounded by warehouses, the area around the dock has been regenerated, and most of the warehouses have now been converted to offices, pubs, and apartments. Most the former warehouse buildings have kept their original names; the building by the lock is predictably called "Lock Warehouse", another one of these erstwhile stores is called "Vinings Warehouse". Attached to this structure is what looks like a very large riveted iron box; presumably meant to represent the hull of an old ship, This edifice is known locally as "The Box on the Docks", situated within this "box" is Vinings Restaurant, serving Pan-Asian Cuisine. Once you set foot inside the "box" you will be pleasantly surprised by the interior; you in no way feel that you have stepped into an enclosed iron tomb, in fact the experience is just the opposite. Along the side of the restaurant, adjacent to the water, instead of the rusting

64

iron sides you are expecting you are presented with a wall made up of a multiple of large glass panes affording a view overlooking the docks basin. If you are surprised by the decor you will be astounded by the selection and quality of the food on offer; if you are ever in Gloucester go to Vinings for a meal, you will not be disappointed.

Happily for the trio on board *Akita*, the "Box on the Docks" was just a short stroll away. A menu had been acquired earlier in the day and a telephone order for a takeaway had been placed, all that remained was to amble over and collect the inevitable white plastic bag that would contain our delicious fare. Stanley was relieved when he smelt and then saw the bag containing our takeaway; he knew that he was not allowed in the restaurant and would not have like being left in the boat on his own!

Sunday morning arrived, heralded by the dawn chorus of the seagulls; I lugged the water jerrycans over to a water point located in the "Barge Arm" and used the BW key (British Waterways) to unlock the tap. With jerrycans filled I struggled back to Cat and Stanley; if only Stanley could carry jerrycans.

We took Stanley for his morning walk on Alney Island, then walked around the quiet docks; it was still early so the crowds to see the day events had not yet materialised and there were very few establishments open. Luckily for us there was a mobile café serving breakfast baps open for business; Dave H. had joined us so with a cautious look around for Ratty and co. we ordered a breakfast roll each then the four of us sat down to eat. Cat, Dave, and I sat at a metal table on lightweight metal chairs, with Stanley settling down on the floor beside me. Now, to remind you, Stanley is a big strong boy, so to make life easier I have an XXL retractable lead and I use an old climbing sling which I wear over my shoulder, and the lead attaches to a karabiner on the sling. This system works well! That is, it works well until you are sitting down on a chair tucking into your breakfast bap and Stanley decides to go for an unsanctioned little walk. I can testify that if this should happen you will at one moment be upright, facing forward, and enjoying your snack and then a moment later feel yourself tipping over backwards to land on your back still in a seated position on your chair and clutching your breakfast roll with egg yolk dripping onto your chest. Furthermore I can attest that this is extremely embarrassing – even though my coolness-enhancing leather hat was still firmly in place I must confess that a certain amount of my composure may have been lost! Stanley did not get a treat from me on this occasion, although I think his diabolical action endeared him to the other customers and passers-by because they all seemed to be smiling! I am told that one day I will see the funny side of this traumatic incident ...

We had planned to leave the Tall Ships Festival and head north through Gloucester Lock so that Cat could experience the River Severn, however, Cat, still not having cruised on the boat, was uneasy about going on the river for her first voyage, so it was decided to chug back to our "home port" and spend Sunday night at the marina. By the time the decision to cruise south had been made it was too late to leave our mooring, due to the Vikings again trying to make off with a now very jaded lady of Gloucester and yet again being apprehended. Some people never learn, but you do have to admire their tenacity! The show continued with the loud bangs of the Royal Marines aboard the Blue Launch firing broadsides at nothing in particular – poor Stanley, if only he could have returned fire!

The show in the basin was temporarily suspended to allow the boating traffic to pass through the docks; there were several boats that had locked up from the river but were still waiting in the large chamber, boats coming from the south were waiting to cruise into the very same lock. Other craft were waiting to leave and return to the private mooring in the Victoria basin and still others, including us aboard *Akita*, were waiting to leave the visitor moorings in the main basin to head both north and south. Thrown into the mix just to make a life even more stimulating, a larger vessel, the *Queen Boadicea II*, was due to cast off, turn around, and head south carrying fee-paying passengers on a cruise! In short it was going to be like a hectic day at Heathrow – we were going to need some kind of air traffic control. This mayhem in the making was rectified by simply opening the lock gates and the bridges and at the same time lighting the blue touch paper then standing back to watch the show!

With next to no control; and a lot of frustrated boaters, some who had been waiting a long time, and did not want to miss the bridges and locks that would surely close before they got there, this was going to be interesting. The hordes of people watching from every inch of the crowded dockside were treated to the best show of the tall ships event: inland waterway boats of every description surged forward to their objectives, all areas of Gloucester Docks basins were awash with boats going in every direction. In to this confused muddle, not wanting to miss the boat while desperately trying to miss other boats, sailed little *Akita* with perhaps the most inexperienced crew of all.

I reversed out of the visitor moorings and swung the bow around towards the south. Cat was sitting on the foredeck and her view changed from looking at the crowds standing outside the dockside pub to being presented with the sight of boats of every type coming and going in every direction – for her this was a most disconcerting introduction to boating! Now I had *Akita* pointing in the correct direction I joined the other skippers who were drifting, waiting for their moment to commit to the melee. I saw a gap in the traffic and set off to exit under the still-open Llanthony Bridge, hoping it would remain raised. I was focused on and heading towards the still-elevated bridge when into view emerged the bulk of *Queen Boadicea II*; she had left her mooring and was heading towards Cat who was still sat in the bow. At this point I did not have a clue what *Boadicea* was going to do so I throttled back waiting to see what would happen and wondered if Cat had her lifejacket on.

Rather disconcertingly for all aboard our little *Akita*, *Queen Boadicea II* went from one side of the docks to the other, at which point I finally realised she planned to turn around (I would later find out this is part of her normal routine). Upon this revelation I pushed the throttle forward to make good our exit from Gloucester Docks and the Tall Ships Festival.

Operation Dynamo and the Dunkirk Little Ships

When writing this book I wanted to stick to the topic and not deviate by filling pages with subjects that have little to do with the inland waterways or boating. I wanted this book to do "exactly what it says on the tin". However, after an admittedly small, and, granted, unscientific poll, I am sad to say that some of the people that I have asked could not tell me what a "Dunkirk Little Ship" is. They shall of course remain nameless (Dave B.)!

This lack of historical knowledge necessitates that I give a very brief description of what happened at Dunkirk and what a "Dunkirk Little Ship" is:

During the Second World War, in mid-1940, the BEF (British Expeditionary Force) and the French Army were retreating from the Germans; the British and French Allies were forced into an ever-decreasing pocket around Dunkirk. There was a plan – code named "Operation Dynamo" – to evacuate the bulk of the British Army and their French allies across the English Channel to England. Part of the plan involved the requisitioning of smaller boats – these became known as the "Dunkirk Little Ships". These smaller boats would be used to take men from the beaches to the larger ships of the Royal Navy. The *Queen Boadicea II,* commanded by Lieutenant J.S. Seal RNR, braved the bombing and went into Dunkirk harbour itself.

During Operation Dynamo some 338,000 British and French Troops were evacuated between the 28th of May and the 4th of June 1940. *Queen Boadicea II* was one of those "Little Ships".

The *Queen Boadicea II* (QB2) was built in 1936, she has a 65-foot steel hull with a beam of 14' 6", and she was originally used as a River Thames passenger boat carrying up to 145 passengers.

The QB2 now resides in Gloucester Docks; she does a forty-five-minute round trip up and down the G&S Canal complete with lively commentary from the captain. If you are ever in Gloucester look her up and maybe even take a cruise on this Dunkirk little ship; just tell the captain to keep a lookout for *Akita*!

Driving Lesson

Once we were underway and away from the Tall Ships Festival; we followed a line of assorted craft south along the G&S Canal while I attempted to educate Cat with the "vast amount" of knowledge I had so far acquired on the finer points of boat handling (this did not take long).

Lesson given, I decided it was time for Cat to take the helm on the open canal, this went well, so, full of pride in my "obvious ability" to train anyone in helmsmanship, I suggested that Cat should attempt to moor for the first time. 'It's OK,' I said, 'I'll talk you through it.'

As we approached the bank with Cat steering, I pulled back the throttle then walked to the other side of the boat to assess the gap between the hard steel pilings at the side of the canal and the delicate hull of *Akita*. When it was time I said to Cat, 'Throttle back and go into reverse,' she did nothing. 'Throttle back, REVERSE!' I shouted. As we bumped and scraped along the side of the canal, I reached across and turned the engine off. We finally came to a rest in what can only be described as a nautical crash landing. While I was wondering just how efficient my newly fitted bilge pumps would be; I realised that perhaps I should have shown Cat where the throttle was!

I stepped ashore and using mooring stakes I secured poor, battered *Akita* to the bank. As I was doing so, Cat said, 'There is something floating in the water just behind us, do you think it had anything to do with us?' I looked over the stern to see one of our fenders bobbing in the water – the poor thing had been ripped off in the impact. Our newly acquired boathook was put to good use, then, after reattaching the forlorn fender, we celebrated my teaching proficiency with a nice mug of tea.

After more tea and taking Stanley for a short walk to pump out his bilge, we cruised towards our home mooring next to Mark's boat in the marina. I hope Mark will not mind me mentioning a little about his boat, *Sequana*: she is a 30-foot centre cockpit cruiser that has seen far better days; she looks like she took a direct hit at the Battle of Jutland, limped home, but was never repaired. I am not sure how Mark can live aboard this floating wreckage but somehow he did manage to survive a very long cold winter in her and he keeps telling me: 'it's a work in progress'. Cans of beer must be vital to the restoration and work must be continuing at a frantic pace as Mark always seems to have a beer in hand; although to date I have seen not any sign of improvement! However, judging by the amount of beer cans being kept cool by floating them in a large fishing net at the stern of the vessel, I am reassured that lots of additional work is planned.

We entered the marina and I could only imagine what poor Mark was thinking as he saw the bows of *Akita* approaching his pride and joy. For my part all I could do was hope that I did not make him homeless as I attempted to insert *Akita* into the small gap between the pontoon and his home. We arrived with our usual finesse, ricocheting between the pontoon and Mark's floating battle memorial before coming to rest with a last little bump. Mark's boat stopped rocking on its ropes and thankfully remained afloat. Mark had a wry smile on his face as he opened another beer: 'Cheers and welcome home!'

Work, Beer and Sopwith Camel vs Swan

When cruising our boat out on the Cut, one of the things I miss is the availability of motorised transportation; you have to plan ahead, take supplies with you on the boat, and know where you are and where shops and curry houses are in relation to both your current location and where you are going to be next time you moor up. Brian, our campervan, was parked at the marina so, taking advantage of the fact that we now had a vehicle at our disposal, we climbed onboard and drove to where else but the local curry house.

The following morning we awoke to the combined aroma of last night's curry and Stanley's posterior emissions (now there is a thought for a weapon of mass destruction). It was time to continue the refurbishment of *Akita*; there were just a few small jobs remaining that could be done by us, so the pace of work was more relaxed than had been the case before the Tall Ships Festival. Even with the eased work rate, Mark said we made him feel guilty about the lack of any discernible progress aboard his boat, and the fact that all the work done on *Akita* thus far had been achieved without the aid of beer! I have been thinking about this, and have come to the conclusion that perhaps beer (unlike curry) is not the best substance for expediting boat repairs. Maybe I should share this revelation with Mark, but I suspect he already knows.

All too soon the bank holiday Monday drew to a close, and, as it did, so the real world rudely imposed itself in to my consciousness. I wanted to try to make it go away, much like you do when you wake from a dream and try to lapse back into sleep, but that never works – the dream is always lost and you are forced to reluctantly emerge back into real life with a sense of loss. This is how I now felt: like a kid coming to terms with the fact that the summer holidays are over and school is beckoning like the grim reaper.

The misery of the working week was only endured by day-dreaming, planning boating trips, and making lists of the little jobs to do on *Akita*. I tried to console myself that it was only another twenty or so years before I could retire but strangely that did not seem to help!

Because of the previous bank holiday the working week was shorter and "Happy Friday" was worked through, so at last I could escape back to Cat, Stanley, and *Akita*.

We were now spending more and more time on *Akita*; even if we were not cruising we would stay at the marina to do odd jobs aboard the boat, we watched other boats arriving at and leaving their moorings and for the most part making a better job at docking than me. Boating people are of course a friendly bunch and people would quite often stop as they were walking by and have an extended chat.

Mark's friends had arrived and judging by the amount of beer cans they had with them it looked like a lot of "work" was about to be undertaken. Cat and I were busying ourselves with some task or other and Stanley was lounging on the pontoon next to *Akita* eyeing the ducks. We heard a conversation punctuated with laughter emanating from the stern of Mark's boat; the talk and merriment did not abate, so, intrigued, I walked to the aft of *Sequana* to see what the jollity was about. Mark was sitting in a small inflatable dinghy to which he and his fellow "workers" were attempting to fit a small outboard motor that looked like it had been salvaged from the wreck of a First World War Sopwith Camel biplane.

Dinghy now fully inflated, and the Sopwith Camel engine mounted, the happy bunch of would-be workers were now struggling to start the motor by pulling hard on a piece of old string, without any success. After much discussion and pulling of string, the engine fired into life for the first time since the First World War and the dinghy shot out into the marina basin with a very surprised and somewhat bemused Mark still aboard. As Mark zigzagged further out into the basin he was shouting that he did not know what he was doing, this only served to make his "friends" laugh even harder.

Once Mark had recovered from the initial shock of being propelled into the open expanse of the marina, he attempted to take control of the small boat as the onlookers, still laughing, shouted advice from the safety of the pontoon. Still not fully in control of the dinghy, Mark was heading directly towards a poor unsuspecting swan which was serenely drifting on the clear water. Swan and inflatable dinghy came together with a glancing blow; Mark looked appalled as laughter radiated from the pontoons, and the swan shuffled its tail feathers as it attempted to regain its dignity. Mark finally managed to close the throttle and retuned towards his friends who were still in hysterics

(*No harm occurred to any animal or birds in the writing of this book*).

Let's Start Using the Boat!

We started to notice vacant moorings in the marina as boats were leaving to cruise the inland waterways network for the summer months. We were chatting to some of the owners and they told us that that would not be returning until September at the earliest. I envied the crews who had the time to do this, and while not wishing my life away, was looking forward to retirement or a lottery win so that I could do the same!

Now that Cat had finally been on the boat, helped crew it, and had a go a steering, I was keen that we should both go for another cruise as soon as possible in order to hone our skills, so I set about planning our next trip. We had taken to cruising the two hours from the marina to a supermarket near to Gloucester Docks to buy our weekly shopping. We would have lunch at The Orchard pub seated outside with Stanley and then make our way back to the marina. These little trips were good fun and it was a novel way to go shopping but I felt that to really make the most of the boat we should be living on it over the weekend away from the marina and that we should get onto the River Severn so that Cat could have her first taste of the river – boating, not drinking!

The plan was to make our way to the Haw Bridge pub, which is approximately eight miles up-river from Gloucester Lock. Yet again because of the restrictive opening hours on the G&S canal we had to plan this simple trip like a military operation. I managed to leave work a little early and rushed home. Cat had Stanley in his harness and they were both sitting in the van with the kit ready for our weekend away. I pulled up on the drive, leaped out of the car and into the campervan and we shot south down the M5 motorway, hoping that there would be no traffic jam. Fortunately the M5 was moving well and we arrived at the marina some twenty-five minutes later. I did the pre-flight checks, started the engine to allow it to warm up, then Cat and I could be seen running to and from the van with our gear and throwing it into the boat. Finally gear, Cat, Dog, and Stressed Bloke aboard I called Junction Bridge on the radio: 'Hello Junction Bridge from *Akita*, over.' The bridge keeper responded and I spoke into the radio to let them know my intentions. 'I would like to leave the marina wind (turn around) in the basin and head north towards Gloucester, over.'

'All understood. I will have the bridge ready for you,' was the answer from the keeper. The time now was 18.30, the first bridge was now out of the way, but we had to get passed Parkend Bridge before it closed at 18.50. Twenty minutes later we went through the bridge with very little time to spare; we could now try to relax. We moored alongside the towpath and took Stanley for his delayed walk.

I knew that it was now the weekend and I was on the canal and that it was time to relax and have fun, but after the stress of the working week and having to go hell for leather to get past the first two low bridges that *Akita* could not fit under I was finding it difficult to wind down. Walk over, we returned to *Akita* and to the chilli that Cat had made during the afternoon. Cat was now using *Akita*'s gas oven for the first time to reheat the chilli and heat up some garlic bread. A lovely meal was served and sitting at the table looking out of the window across the wide ship canal on this beautiful summer's evening I at last started to readjust to the slower pace of life and began to chill out.

Cat, Stanley and *Akita*

We were aware that the bridges were now all closed; however, unlike the two bridges that we had already passed through, Sellars, Rea, Sims, and Netheridge Bridges are higher and so Akita could past underneath them before having to stop and wait for the very low Hempsted Bridge to open at eight o' clock on Saturday morning. Meal over and dishes done we continued towards Gloucester and came to the first of the now-closed bridges, the keeper was long gone and the traffic lights switched off, so the drill was simple: you approach and pass under the bridge with caution, this method was repeated at each of the bridges and in the failing light it was time to find a spot alongside the towpath to moor for the night.

This would be our first ever night moored overnight alongside the towpath in the middle of nowhere and not at a pontoon in a marina or the Docks basin. We were a little bit picky about where we wanted to stop; Cat wanted short grass on the bank (think manicured lawn), I did not want to stop on a corner and did want to get as close to Gloucester as possible to save time in the morning. We kept going, passing several likely places on the way, and it was almost dark when we finally stopped.

We tied up with a combination of mooring stakes and piling chains and settled down for our first night of "wild camping" on the boat. All was well for the first hour or two but then the wind must have picked up and *Akita* started to move on her ropes; the gentle swaying was quite nice to start with but then came a noise that rivalled even Stanley's snoring; it sounded like something was going to come through the side of the fibreglass hull.

Thinking that the hull was about to implode I jumped out of bed, donned trousers, and rushed outside to see what was trying to destroy our boat. I could not see what the problem was, so I moved some fenders around, loosened the mooring ropes and returned to bed. Desperate that Cat should enjoy her first night aboard the boat out on the Cut, I said, 'That did the trick.' Cat did not seem impressed with my declaration that all was well, and as it turned out she was right!

Another two hours went by and all *was* well, then the noise retuned in earnest. At first I tried to ignore it and just hoped it would just go away again but it became more constant and it seemed that real damage would occur. Once more I climbed out of bed (why does it always have to be the bloke?) and made my way outside this time clutching a boathook. To add to my joy it had started to rain, great!

I prodded along the side of boat between the hull and the bank with the boathook and this time found the problem: there was a small tree hidden in the long grass, someone had cut the branches off and the stumps were now gaining their revenge on the human race by trying to break through *Akita*'s hull. There was no choice – I would have to move to another location.

It was two o'clock in the morning, pouring with rain, and I was manually pulling *Akita* with Cat and Stanley still aboard down the Cut looking for another place to moor – one with a manicured lawn and no homicidal zombie trees. Once *Akita* had been relocated I set about securing her back to the bank. You will not believe how loud the sound is when a hammer hits a mooring stake at two in the morning! I climbed back onboard saying, 'That did the trick.' Cat's silence was all the comment I needed to let me know how she felt. (Another lesson learnt!)

Even with the lack of a good night's sleep we were feeling pretty good when Stanley woke us for his walk. The normal morning routine was adhered to and once we had refuelled from the garage with the sinking pontoon we were in time to follow the first boat through the now-open Hempstead and Llanthony Bridges and into Gloucester Lock.

I had briefed Cat on what to expect and what to do in the river locks so it was with confidence that we sailed into what would be Cat's first ever lock. True to form the routine in the lock had changed; instead of looping a rope through the vertical cable running down the side of the chamber, the lock-keeper asked for our ropes which he looped over a bollard on top of the lock. I knew that our mooring ropes were probably not going to be long enough for the sixteen-foot drop, particularly the bow line, and so quick as a flash Cat and I changed positions with her taking the rope at the stern and me at the bow. The gate closed and the water level dropped and we fed out the ropes; by the time we were at river level at the bottom of the chamber I was on tiptoes standing on the foredeck wall. Another lesson learnt: always have long ropes handy on the bow and stern when going on the river!

With the minor stress in Gloucester Lock over, I

cruised out onto the River Severn with Cat on board for the first time. We zigzagged our way up to the Upper Parting and emerged onto the more exposed wider part of the river. The wind had picked up and the river had white spray blowing from the top of the waves, but little *Akita*'s bow cut through them and pushed her way forward against the flow of the river without a care. Both Cat and I were really starting to like our boat and were getting to be quite proud of her.

We continued heading upstream and I pointed out some of the critical navigation points to Cat; I had told her all about these points before, but I think she just thought this was boring "Man's stuff" and I don't think she was listening. However, after I told her that she would be taking the wheel she now *was* paying attention and even asked me to repeat a few things, nothing like the possibility of sinking a boat to get someone's attention!

We had phoned the inn at Haw Bridge in advance to make sure Stanley was permitted inside; so certain in the knowledge that we were going to get a good meal indoors for once, we moored at the very good pontoons outside the Haw Bridge Inn. Once Stanley had had a little walk to do the "necessary" Cat did the recon inside the pub to secure a table and check the place out for other dogs.

Once we were settled, Cat went to the bar to order chicken and chips in a basket (I had not had that for years!). The staff could not have been friendlier and made a big fuss of Stanley. The meal was great and if you have a dog, boat, or both, I would recommend the Haw Bridge Inn for a good bar meal.

We left the mooring and turned around to follow the river downstream. As the wind had increased, I was worried that Cat would feel nervous because the waves were crashing against the hull but she sat on the foredeck and really seemed to be enjoying herself, even when spray from some of the larger waves splashed over the bow onto her. *Akita* took all this in her stride and both Cat and I felt at ease on the river in our little boat; *Akita* was built for this!

We were very surprised when in what seemed no time at all we arrived back at the Upper Parting; it is a lot quicker coming down-river! We made our way along the East Channel and locked up into Gloucester Docks, this time roping onto the vertical cables.

The VHF radio again paid for itself – an announcement was broadcast stating that because of the strengthening wind some of the bridges on the G&S, including Llanthony, were now closed. The bridge closures effectively trapped us in Gloucester Docks Basin so we were left with no option other than to moor for Saturday night outside Fosters for another very noisy night by the pub, followed by an early morning alarm call from the irritating seagulls. Although the moorings in the docks are very good, we both vowed that we would try not to overnight there again; it really is too loud and not conducive to a good night's sleep.

By the morning the wind had subsided and we were able to leave the docks as soon as the bridges started to operate at 08.00 and make our way back to Saul Junction. Sunday came to an end and work once again beckoned, but I consoled myself with the fact that we both were enjoying the boat and at least I could live for the weekends.

With the lessons learnt in the lock, I ordered a 50-metre rope which was cut in half so we now had a 25-metre rope for both the fore and stern decks. These ropes have proved to be very useful since!

While I am on the subject of ropes, I should mention the "Centre Line" or "Lazy Line", this long rope is very handy and essential if you are cruising singlehanded. The centre line is typically attached to a centre point on the cabin roof, it is then run back along the roof and should be positioned so that it can be easily reached from both sides of the boat from the stern deck. When you are going to moor you can step ashore grabbing the centre line as you go, this rope can then be used to control the boat and even tie up with temporarily; you should then secure the boat with the bow and stern lines. The centre line can also be used to help you control your boat in locks.

One word of warning: make sure your centre line is securely attached to your boat. The last thing you want to do is to step onto the bank, flick your centre line over any obstacles that may be on the roof, and have the line detach from the boat, as you then watch your vessel drift away from the bank like the *Mary Celeste*!

Whenever I am stepping on or off the boat I am always conscious of what I have in my pockets – the last thing I want is to have something fall out and in to the Cut. If my pockets have zips I try to make sure they are closed.

My boat keys are on a cork float which in theory should stop them from sinking should I drop them in to the water, but I suspect that I have too many keys attached so the combined weight might just drag the poor float down into the abyss.

Something that is handy to keep aboard a boat is a powerful magnet attached to a length of strong cord, so if you do manage to drop something that is attracted to a magnet, you at least stand a chance of retrieving it. You can purchase a "Sea Magnet" from most chandleries.

Wisdom, Weeds and Weil's Disease

As a novice on the waterways one of the most stressful things is not knowing what you are doing and what is going on around you; this is easily remedied by firstly a little bit of research and secondly gaining experience.

Although a lot of boats have radios, not all do; so knowing what the blasts from other vessels' horns mean is very handy, likewise it is also good to inform other crafts of your intention (don't be embarrassed to use your horn!):

1 Extra LONG blast – Warning at blind bends, tunnels and junctions.

1 blast – Going to the RIGHT.

2 blasts – Going to the LEFT.

3 blasts – Trying to STOP or go BACKWARDS (engine going astern).

4 blasts, pause, then 1 blast – Turning round to the RIGHT.

4 blasts, pause, then 2 blasts – Turning round to the LEFT.

1 long blast then 2 short blasts – I can't manoeuvre.

5 or more short blasts – Your (the other vessel's)

intentions are unclear.

Channel Markings

Cruising DOWN stream – RED markers to your RIGHT.
Green to your LEFT.

Cruising UP stream – RED markers to your LEFT
Green to your RIGHT.

Traffic Lights

Note: Always check with the local waterway that you are
on – some operate a different system (see below).

RED – Stop (do not pass this light).

RED + GREEN – Get ready to go (but do not pass this
light).

GREEN – Go.

AMBER – Proceed with caution.

The locks and bridges on the River Severn and Gloucester
& Sharpness Canal operate their own traffic lights system:

Red – STOP, do not enter the lock/pass the light or go
through the bridge.

Flashing Red – The lock-/bridge-keeper has seen you, but
you still need to STOP.

Green – Go, you may enter the lock/pass through the
bridge.

When passing dredgers or other works; pass on the side showing GREEN or WHITE shapes or lights, DO NOT PASS ON THE SIDE SHOWING RED!

Call me sad, but I keep a laminated crib sheet of the above on the door near to the helm on *Akita*.

Due to other commitments over the following few weeks we were unable to get away in *Akita* for a full weekend and we had to be content with mini cruises up and down the G&S. It was on one of these mini cruises while waiting for a bridge to open that the propeller became fouled. I was over to the right-hand side of the Cut waiting for a green light. There must have been long weeds that took the opportunity to tangle themselves around the slow-moving prop. Once the traffic light switched from red to green I pushed the throttle forward – the engine made its usual noise but *Akita* was hardly moving. I was in an awkward position blocking the bridge with other boats at *Akita*'s stern waiting to follow me through. I had little choice other than to limp past the bridge and then pull over as soon as possible. I shouted over to the bridge-keeper to let him know I had a problem and moored as soon as I had cleared the structure. With the engine turned off and the key removed, I opened the cover and peered through the surprisingly clear water at the prop. I could see nothing untoward but I still used the boathook to prod ineffectually at the propeller. After a minute or so of prodding and poking I restarted the engine and engaged gear; *Akita* surged forward, the prop was clear. I don't think I had cleared it by prodding about with the hook; I think whatever was fouling the prop was untangled and thrown clear when I engaged reverse to bring *Akita* into the bank (another lesson learnt: if your prop is fouled try a burst of reverse to clear it). I really needed to find out how to lift the engine/propeller so that I could inspect the prop!

On a traditional narrowboat access to the propeller is gained through the weed-hatch, a steel cover is removed, usually by undoing thumbscrew-type clamps, you can then reach down through the hatch to check the prop for damage and disentangle anything that is fouling it. However, you have to be careful! You should always remove the key from the ignition then keep it with you so the engine cannot be started. Also care should be taken when probing with hands around the propeller, there could be sharp edges and you never know what is going to be down there, nasty items could include barbed wire and fishing line complete with hooks! Once the inspection is complete the cover should then be secured and then hands should always be washed to prevent Weil's disease.

Weil's disease is spread by rats in the water. There is minimal risk of infection, however, if you develop flu-like symptoms within two to four weeks of dealing with canal or standing water, tell your doctor that you have had contact with canal water and you may want to mention Weil's disease. But both Cat and I always try to wash our hands after handling ropes and always before meals. We find having a bottle of hand sanitizer near to the fore and stern decks is useful.

I went on the boat-handling course but in truth it was a bit late; I had learnt a lot during the "baptism of fire" on our maiden voyage home and on subsequent mini cruises up and down the G&S and the River Severn. Every time I went out in *Akita* I learnt a little more. I have learnt that although wind is a nuisance when you are trying to travel slowly, you can also use it to your advantage, to help you turn. If the wind is gusting when I am leaving my home mooring, I have learnt to put the stern into it first in order to turn around. (However, I still crash into Mark's boat most times I return to our mooring!)

The points I have learnt are small but when added together they equate to a modest understanding of boating

– the result makes life on the water easier and the sum total equals enjoyment.

The fact that I was confined to short cruises gave me time to continue with some of the little jobs that still needed to be completed and make some small changes to things to make living aboard easier. We were also planning our next weekend away which would be a short trip to visit Tewkesbury.

Tewkesbury, Unlucky for the Unicorn

Finally we had a full weekend to ourselves, and with the arrival of Friday evening our plan for the excursion to Tewkesbury swung in to action. Once again, due to the restrictive opening hours on the G&S; we had to race to get past the first two bridges, it was when this was narrowly achieved that we made a big mistake! We (meaning me) elected to keep going, totally forgetting that poor Stanley had not had his walk. Cat screamed, 'Oh no, we have a major problem!' My first thought was that we were taking on water but thankfully this was not the case. Poor Stanley really needed to "go" and having no other choice he had done so all over the foredeck – in all fairness to him he had picked the best spot possible! I considered this incident my fault so while Cat steered one *Akita* I cleared up after the other.

We cruised as far as we could but once we arrived at Hempsted Bridge we were left with no option but to bed down for the night and wait for the bridge to open in the morning. Saturday morning dawned; the bridge was opened in good time, and we continued under the High Orchard Bridge and approached the distinctively red painted lightship *Sula*.

Sula, originally named with the catchy moniker of 'SPURN LV14' served as a lightship on the River Humber between the years 1959 and 1985. After 1985 the ship had a few owners before undergoing a three-year refit at

Sharpness Docks. She was then towed to her permanent moorings at Gloucester. *Sula* is now used as a centre for alternative therapies and is also a Buddhist Centre. You can step onboard where tea, coffee, and cakes are served on deck or inside if the weather is inclement. *Sula* has also become a local tourist attraction but is only fully open to the public during events such as the heritage weekend and the Gloucester Tall Ships Festival.

We continued past the lightship and onto the service pontoon by Llanthony Bridge. I had to empty the porta-potty (it's a crap job but someone had to do it) and then fill up the water jerrycans. By the time I had walked the full length of the pontoon with a filled 25-litre jerrycan in each hand, my arms were a lot longer and the rest of me shorter! Another lesson learnt, time to get a sack truck!

As we were stowing the last of the jerrycans onboard; a convoy of boats was heading north towards Llanthony Bridge. We were now getting proficient at mooring and casting off, so in quick time and with no stress, I informed the bridge- and lock-keepers of our intention via the radio and we joined the back of the convoy. We had a green light for both the bridge and lock; we cruised slowly inside, our normal mooring lines and the newly acquired long ropes to hand. The lock-keeper instructed us to rope to the bollards at the top of the lock; so feeling smug that we had learnt from experience and we had the foresight to have the long ropes ready we did as instructed. We were lowered to river level, the gates were opened, Cat pushed the bow away from the lock wall with a short boat-pole (so she did not have to touch the "slimy wall" with her delicate little hands), I pushed the stern away and we cruised out of the lock feeling like professionals. Through teamwork we were getting a system going and the river locks were getting easier.

We had a nice cruise up-river on the Severn and stopped off at very good moorings at the Lower Lode

Hotel where we had yet another great riverside pub meal (and yes dogs are very welcome).

We continued onto the Upper Lode Lock and after a short wait outside with another narrowboat we were admitted in and roped to the vertical cables. Locks can be sociable places and as the chamber was filling we chatted to the couple on the other boat. I had seen this boat out on the water a few times before – it had a picture of three cats on the side and a little cat statue on the front, I asked if they had any real cats on board. The man replied saying they still had two cats but used to have three, unfortunately one of the cats was shot by someone hunting foxes who then grabbed the body of the poor fallen pet and ran off with it. (Some people are so cruel.)

Parting company with the River Severn we turned right and headed eastwards on the Old River Avon for the first time. Looking ahead I could not believe what I was seeing and I had to look through my monocular to clarify what I thought I saw. Perched on top of an elevated wall 20 or so foot up, very high and dry and at a precarious angle was the 57-foot narrowboat *Unicorn*. Apparently the boat had been swept from its mooring in autumn floods the previous year and was still waiting for its owner to arrange recovery (and this was mid-July).

We only had a short way to go up the Old Avon to the spot where I intended to moor overnight. However, there was only one place to tie up and this was totally unsuitable, the dockside wall was at the same height as *Akita*'s roof and there was no way poor Stanley could get off the boat. Leaving Cat and Stanley aboard I climbed up onto the quayside and walked to see Bob, the keeper of the Avon Lock. Bob turn out to be very helpful (as most keepers seem to be); he suggested that we lock up to the River Avon itself and there we would find good moorings. The cost for locking through was minimal, so putting our new ropes to work once again we proceeded through and found a good mooring for the night next to Healing's Mill just up-river for Quay Street Bridge and close, but not too close, to the stricken narrowboat *Unicorn*.

Unicorn was to my eyes a bit of an eyesore, however, because of its odd and dramatic position it turned out to be a bit an attraction. Worryingly, part of the fence protecting the area had been removed and to my surprise "adults" were sitting on the ground underneath the boat having a picnic. This in itself was dumb but then another so-called adult walked up to the rudder and threw his entire body weight against it in an effort to move it. Luckily the boat did not move; but you do not have to think too hard about what the consequences would have been if it had!

Ever the one to have a mixed and balanced diet, I decided to forgo my curry in favour of a pepperoni and chicken pizza. Stanley helped clean up by removing the topping of his piece of pizza and leaving the now soggy bread base on the floor for me to tread on with bare feet on a trip to the loo in the middle of the night. Lovely!

Akita's shower was still not working – so far this had not been a problem because we had been making use of the shower facilities at the marina and at Gloucester Docks. However, no such amenities were available near to our current location. It had been a hot and sticky day and I wanted a wash before settling down for the night. I evicted the porta-potty from the shower tray and, making use of some hot water from the kettle, a couple of flannels, and a bowl, I had a strip wash. On a practical note – having a strip wash is a great way of saving water if you have a limited supply.

The following morning, after peeling pizza base from my hitherto clean foot, I took Stanley for a walk on the Severn Ham Common. The "Ham" is an island made up of a wide expanse flat grassland surrounded by the rivers Severn, Old Avon, and the Avon; this is another great place to walk your dog, but be warned, sometimes there are sheep grazing, also the Ham Common is liable to flood if the rivers are in spate. Cat stayed aboard *Akita* and had a lie-in, perhaps one day I too will get a chance to do this …

Lock Crazy

We locked back down and cruised out on the River Severn and approached Upper Lode Lock with confidence – after all we now had a system, we were experienced – what could go wrong?

We entered the lock and were coming in lined up perfectly to rope up to the cables on the lock wall. I was feeling smug; I was showing others how to do it, straight in, rope up, job done. Cat's screams snapped me out of my self-congratulations – I looked to see what she was pointing at, and to my horror saw there was a terrified duck in the rapidly narrowing gap between the lock wall and *Akita*'s hull. I slammed the boat into reverse, swung the wheel over, and hoped the duck would make good its escape. It went forward but seeing Cat it changed its mind, turned around and came back toward the stern. It then saw me and went back toward Cat. This was like playing tennis with a duck; I had no choice but to swing *Akita*'s stern away from the wall so the Daffy could make good her escape. So much for a smooth entry into the lock!

Other vessels followed us in to the lock; a narrowboat, and, looking rather out of place in this large river lock, a man in a canoe. I felt compelled to tell them about the incident with duck to avoid looking like a total idiot who could not control his boat! Lock filled, we manage to make amends by making a perfect exit through the open gates.

One of the things I like about boating is that if you are

not the one doing the steering you are pretty much free to do as you will; you can make tea, cook/eat food, use the loo, have a wash, or even go to sleep. It is nice to close your eyes in one place and when you wake up the scenery has totally changed.

Retracing our steps (or wake) back down the Severn, Cat was busy with her brand new camera taking a photo of anything and everything while I steered, after a while she came to the stern and asked if I would like a break. Grabbing the rare opportunity to have a "break" I quickly agreed and relinquished the wheel only to be told to put the kettle on and make tea for the new captain!

Tea made, drunk and mugs swilled, I settled down on the bed to have a well-deserved snooze. I was off in the land of nod when there was a loud bang. I was instantly awake and jumped off the bed thinking we had hit something, but then I saw that we had only run into the wake of a large cruiser that had just passed us going in the opposite direction, perhaps a bit too quickly. Trying to slow my heart-rate I climbed back onto the bed in order to make my way back to the land of dreams when Cat called me back to the stern and the wheel – so much for my "break"!

We had agreed to pick up some passengers (my relatives) from the pontoon at Ashleworth Court and run them back down to Gloucester for a mini pleasure cruise. We managed to time our arrival about right and they were waiting for us as we turned around and headed back into the current to moor. Once they, and as it turned out, their dog, were aboard we turned back around and continued down-river. Cat took the helm while I barricaded the gangway to prevent any altercation between Stanley and our new four-legged passenger.

I was standing on the foredeck chatting to our passengers when the conversation died in my throat; coming up-river towards us was another vessel and it looked like a mirror image of our boat (but maybe a bit tidier). As we drew closer, both crews were waving and taking photos of each other's boats. I had never seen another craft like *Akita* on the water and what made it really strange is that both very similar vessels were named after dogs – ours *Akita* and theirs was called *Greyhound*. We parted company and I for my part was regretting the fact that we did not get a chance to have a chat to the other crew, and have a quick peek inside their nice-looking boat!

Using the VHF radio, Gloucester Lock was called from the Upper Parting and assurances were given about the readiness of the lock. I also enquired about traffic coming up-river toward us. Happy that the only inbound vessels on the narrow winding section of the river were narrowboats and cruisers, we carried on towards Gloucester Lock with me at the helm. As it turned out there were a lot of boats coming the other way and I reflected that if I had met this many boats on this section of river two months ago I would have had a meltdown, but now I was taking it in my stride.

As we neared Gloucester we caught up with a narrowboat and followed her into the lock. She was directed to the port side of the lock, this is the less turbulent side when the lock is filling. I looked up and saw that the keeper was directing me to the starboard side – I knew this to be the more turbulent region but was unfazed by it, we would simply rope up and hold on tight. As I was lining up to head over to the right-hand side the keeper then seemed to change his mind and I realised that he wanted *Akita* to breast up with the other narrowboat. We breasted up with no problems and were directed to hold onto the roof handrail of the narrowboat. 'This is novel,' I said to the other boater as he stood at the stern of his boat and he agreed. The gates were closed and as the paddles were opened the water rush in, it was indeed turbulent; Cat and I struggled to hold the two boats together as the water level was raised. This method of lock usage was new to us and was not that enjoyable. But it was an experience and if we have to do it again at least we know what to expect.

Our passengers disembarked and we took the opportunity to take Stanley for a walk so he could "offload" to avoid any repeat of his little accident of the outbound journey.

Cat offered to steer so that I could have another "break". I stepped into the cabin heading towards the bed to continue my earlier snooze. Cat then decided that this would be a good time for me to carry on with some little tasks on the boat. As the sun beat down and we cruised south along the G&S, I found myself replacing the black cable ties that held the blinds in place with white ones because as Cat said, 'they would look better'. I always find my little "breaks" so relaxing!

We had once again made good time down-river and had a clear run on the G&S, and two hours later *Akita* was back at her home mooring tied up safely resplendent with new white cable ties holding the blinds in place.

The mooring next-door-but-one to us had been vacant for the whole time that we had been at the marina, but now there was a boat occupying the space. Our new neighbours once removed were on their boat and I got talking to them. They had only just started to use their boat and it seemed that they would have to go through the same learning curve that I had. We chatted and, as we did, I realised how much I had learnt over the last few months; I tried to give them some useful hints and tips, mindful that this could quickly turn into information overload.

The remainder of a very pleasant Sunday evening was spent at the marina chatting to Mark, drinking tea, and eating the Chinese takeaway that Cat had procured.

One of the features in our, and other, marinas, are the trolleys that are left at strategic places throughout the site; boaters use these trolleys to transfer items from their cars along the pontoons to the boats and back. You can almost tell if it is a Friday or a Sunday from the direction that the articles are being transported: Towards the boat = Friday, towards the car = Sunday. When I see the loads heading towards the cars I always feel a little sad because I know the weekend is coming to an end!

Never the Same Twice

We were now spending every weekend at the marina or cruising out on the cut or river. The little tweaks and changes that were done made living within the confined space in the boat easier – whether it was something as simple as adding hooks for a towel or a coat, or replacing the small ex-campervan table for a full-size one, all these things added up to make living aboard more enjoyable.

We had taken to walking Stanley on a circular walk outside the marina. Along the G&S and Stroud Water Canals, we were doing the same walk every time but were still enjoying it and were not getting bored with what could have been a repetitive routine. The reason for this was simple: each time we went for our stroll the scenery had changed, there were always different crafts sailing along the canal passing through the bridges that were swung open for them. The visitor moorings were in a constant state of flux with different vessels moored alongside the towpath each time we ambled past. We would exchange the odd word or two with other boaters and someone would always comment on Stanley. As we walked along we would point out certain boats and remark on their features, a clever name or sometimes say to each other, 'One day that's what we'll get.' But for the time being we were happy with our little *Akita*.

On early morning walks I can usually tell if I am the first person to walk any given route by the number of cobwebs that seem to wrap themselves around my face; I'm like a walking cobweb magnet! Quite often I can be seen clawing at air around my head – I must look like I suffer from paranoia as I attempt to remove the silky strands from my face and hair. I do not think that I am popular with spiders or maybe they *are* trying to catch me ...

On one such walk, Stanley (as dogs do) was doing the usual stop, sniff, spray, sprint forward again in search of the next interesting smell. I would walk along only to be brought to an abrupt halt by the lead as Stanley stopped suddenly or ran back to investigate some aroma with his nose. This would happen so often that I would rarely look back to see what had attracted him. On one occasion after a prolonged pause, I could hear laughter. I looked round to see Stanley staring intently through the window of a moored narrowboat, while the amused occupants were in fits of laughter. He must have looked very funny with his big "bear head" as he gawked at them through their window.

On some of our walks we would meet people, usually other boaters, and they would start talking to us, say something like, 'Hello, we meet again', while we desperately tried to place them. I am always embarrassed because I'm useless with names and faces and rarely know where I am supposed to know them from (sorry if this was you!). It usually turns out that we have moored next to them at some stage and they always seem to remember us – it may be because we have a relatively unusual boat and we are made even more distinctive by the fact that Stanley is always trotting along with us. Most other people don't have such a memorable dog to aid us in remembering them, but we are still embarrassed when we don't recognise people we have met before.

On some of our walks we will meet people on a regular basis but we will only know them by their dog's name, it's a funny old world when you are an owner of a dog!

Hungry – Need to Eat!

One Saturday we cruised south along the G&S and moored at Sharpness. We were planning to walk to the local hotel for lunch. We arrived early in the afternoon, then we phoned the hotel only to find out that they did not start to serve food until the evening (I am not sure what the residents were meant to eat). Both Cat and I were feeling hungry; so with a new plan in place we started to walk along the towpath to find the local shops. A short distance later we were walking through Sharpness Marina and in no time we found ourselves chatting to fellow boaters. One kind couple produced a drinking bowl for Stanley and while he was drinking his water we asked them how far it was to the local store. They informed that it was quite a walk, seeing that we were by now very hungry we decided to go back to *Akita* to see what food we had on board. It turned out that there was not much to eat on the boat so with plummeting blood sugar levels we pulled up mooring stakes and headed north in search of food. Another lesson learnt *always* have some emergency food aboard. (Curry in cans would be good.)

We returned all the way to Saul Junction but instead of going directly into the marina we stopped at the visitor moorings between Sandfield and Junction Bridges. We had heard on the grapevine (Mark told us) that The Ship Inn did good food; we had phoned ahead to make sure that they were serving food and of course to make sure that no one would jump ship if we turned up with Stanley. Well-behaved dogs were welcome, so we followed some little arrow signs indicating "Ship Inn, accommodation" along a grassy public footpath and over a few stiles. Stanley is a BIG lad and the brave fellow was squeezing himself through the gaps in the stiles that were meant for much smaller dogs. I really wish that whoever constructs stiles would take into consideration large dogs; there has been many a time when we have had to turn back due to an encounter with a non-large-dog-friendly obstacle, I consider these non-dog-friendly stiles to be discrimination against owners of large dogs – we like to walk in the countryside too! (I feel a call to my MP coming on!)

At one stile poor Stanley tried to fit through and almost made it but the top of his harness got caught and he reversed out and made a little crying noise to indicate his displeasure. We removed the harness and after a little encouragement the brave not-so-little boy squeezed his way through, well done, Stanley! Up to this point the grass had been mowed but now the path was un-kept and overgrown to beyond waist height. As Stanley and I forged ahead through this minor jungle, all we could hear from behind was Cat (who was wearing shorts) making little crying noises to indicate her displeasure!

We arrived at the Ship just as it started to rain, we were relieved that unlike the stiles the staff at the Ship were friendly towards dogs and that we were able to be seated in the dry. By this time we were both starving so our meals were eaten with desperation rather than enjoyment – which was a shame because I am sure the food was really quite good! It had been a long day without food (really must get some curry in a can on the boat); we were both feeling tired so leaving the inn we walked back to *Akita,* this time taking the road to avoid the discriminating stiles.

Drips and Tight Ropes

It was pouring with rain and the three of us were soaked to the skin by the time we boarded *Akita*. Using the radio, I called Junction Bridge to let them know that we did not need the bridge opening for us, and we were given the green light to proceed into the marina. The rain was very heavy and I was especially thankful that we had not lost our roof by colliding with Rea Bridge on that first journey home. Other narrowboats were still out on the Cut and the helmsmen were getting soaked as they stood stoically at their tillers. Some held umbrellas or had tied them to the tiller, while others were huddled under large parasols that were, until an hour or so ago, used to shelter from the sun.

This was the first time that I had cruised *Akita* in any substantial rain and I was steering by attentively squinting through the windscreen and lifting the side cover and peering around the flank of the boat. Thankfully we did not have far to go and as luck would have it there was no wind, so within minutes we were approaching our home mooring. Mark's tender (the one with the Sopwith Camel engine) was tied to the stern of *Sequana* and had drifted into our path. Cat, who was looking like a drowned cat, was standing on the foredeck and she simply pushed it aside with the boat pole and we arrived home with an imperceptible bump.

As we were both soaking wet, we made use of the marina showers and then an umbrella to remain dry as we made our way back to the boat. The rain was intensifying, becoming persistent, and flood warnings had been issued. So far it had been a glorious summer and as a result the water level in the canal had dropped a little. So, mindful that all this rain would refill the canal, I made sure the mooring lines were loose.

Cat was making up the bed and I commented that I would not be surprised if we found a leak or two with all the water running over the top of the boat; a minute later the first of the drops landed on her arm, finding its way through one of the screws holding the handrail to the roof. I was ready for this with a screwdriver and a silicon gun and after one other leak was found we were watertight once again. We both agreed that it was lucky that we were there at this time to find and fix leaks.

I have found that having tools and spares on board the boat is essential; there is always some little job or other that needs doing to make life aboard easier. Also things do break and if they are not repaired when you first spot them something is going to fail at an inappropriate, inconvenient, or dangerous time. Boat maintenance is just as, if not more important than maintaining a car; if your car stops you can always pull over and if necessary call the AA or RAC for a tow home. If your boat engine stops on a fast-flowing river things can get a whole lot more complicated!

There is an organisation called "River and Canal Rescue", they are similar to the AA or RAC but service users of the waterways, like their road-based counterparts they offer various levels of cover which you may want to consider.

Bed made and remaining dry, we settled down to listen to the rain hammering on the newly sealed roof; there is something really nice about this sound and it is yet another thing I like about boating … as long as you don't have to go out in it!

The following morning the weather had cleared and, as I was getting out of the boat to take Stanley for his morning walk, I was surprised to note that the mooring ropes were as tight as guitar strings, I released them and *Akita* rose up in the water by a few inches. Another lesson learnt, leave mooring ropes slacker than you think necessary or check your ropes during the night, or better still, do both!

If it Can Go Wrong it Will Go Wrong!

We had arranged to meet Caroline, a friend of Cat's, and give her a trip in the boat. I thought it would be nice to take a cruise on the River Severn. This meant that I would have to be at Gloucester Lock in the early part of the morning in order to make the most of our day out on the river and still get back to the marina on the same day.

Once again because of the restrictive opening hours of the locks and bridges, I had to rush home from work, and then get to the marina ASAP in order to get *Akita* as close to Gloucester as I could the evening before. I arrived home, put some kit into the van, encouraged Stanley to jump into the back, and we were off flying down the M5. As we arrived at the marina there was a very unpleasant odour and I assumed that a farmer had spread some muck or that Stanley had a bad case of flatulence. Once parked, I open the side sliding door of the campervan only to be greeted by the foul smell again; Stanley did indeed have a bad case of something but it was a lot more substantial that mere wind! The "messy not so little accident" had to be cleaned up from the back of my van, and four poo bags and some time later, that I could ill afford, I was ready to warm the boat engine up while I loaded the kit into *Akita*.

The wind was fairly strong but I was confident that I could get the boat out of the marina without incident; I selected reverse and as soon as the bow was clear of the pontoon did a perfect 180-degree turn and selected forward gear. It was at this point that the engine cut out.

The wind pushed *Akita* across the marina while I desperately tried to restart the engine, to no avail, then came the inevitable slow-motion crash into an adjacent pontoon. This was very embarrassing; I really was hoping that my days of drifting of control into things were over! I had put in the time practising, I been on the boat-handling course, and I had a plan for getting out of the marina in the windy conditions which was going well! However, the wind was now pinning me against the pontoon and I was looking like a total amateur through no fault of my own, all because the engine had cut out and would not restart! I lifted the engine cover and quickly found the problem, OK, so it was my fault!

Earlier, when I started the engine to let it warm up, I had knocked the retaining clip on the fuel line; the line had remained attached while the motor was warming up but once I started to manoeuvre the line had detached and the motor stopped shortly thereafter. Luckily for me the fuel line self-seals so there was no fire or any pollution!

I now had the fuel line securely reconnected, I restarted the engine and tried to manoeuvre away from the pontoon. However, due to the warm sunny weather the weeds in the marina had grown with the speed of Jack's beanstalk and proliferated with the enthusiasm of randy rabbits, these weeds now wrapped themselves around *Akita*'s propeller so I had to untangle them from the prop before trying to push the boat away from the pontoon with the wind pushing against me. With a lot of help from another boater I managed to get underway but I knew something was not quite right. I had no choice, I had to keep going or I would not get past the first two bridges before they closed!

Having just made it past the second bridge in time, I stopped to let Stanley have a bit of a walk before having a good dig around the prop with the boathook to make sure all the weeds were clear. I pushed *Akita* out well away from the bank and this time the wind assisted me. I waited until I was out in the centre of the canal before engaging gear in an effort to avoid the weeds grabbing the prop.

It took another hour to get to my next objective, the filling station. I tied up and grabbed the fuel tank then made my way over to the pumps only to find out the garage had closed half an hour earlier. This was typical of how my day was going, but it was not really a problem as I was planning to moor and sleep on the boat in this area so I would just leave *Akita* where she was.

I took Stanley for a proper walk alongside the canal; I could hear the distant rumble of thunder, there was a storm coming our way. We were at the halfway point in our walk and as we were crossing Netheridge Bridge we were given a spectacular display of fork-lightning; the storm was getting closer.

A minute or so later Stanley decided that this would be a good time to sit down for a nice little rest. I explained to him that given the fact that there was a storm coming perhaps this was not the best time or place to stop. He responded to my logic by adopting the prone position and then rolling over for a tummy rub! 'This is not helping!' I told him. 'Up, up!' I pleaded, still no movement. I used every trick in the book to get him moving, to no avail. So I just sat down beside him and waited for the rain.

As soon as I sat down, Stanley deemed that it was time to move on (bloody dog!) We made good time walking north up the path that runs alongside Bristol Road and as we were approaching the garage the rain came – there was no spot or two as a warning, it just instantly rained like you would not believe. The boat was only twenty metres away but there was no way we could make it without getting soaked, and possibly drowning on dry land.

We took cover under the garage forecourt roof to wait out the storm. The wind was driving the rain under the high roof from one side of the forecourt to the other and we were struggling to remain dry even under the cover of the roof. The rain was so intense even the roof could not manage and it started to leak in several places. Bristol Road was instantly flooded as the drains could not cope with the sudden downpour; passing cars had slowed right down and their windscreen wipers were on full speed as drivers leant forward in their seats straining to see through the deluge; this was a real mini monsoon!

After ten minutes the torrent of water falling from the sky eased to what would pass for normal rain. Stanley and I made a break for the dry interior of *Akita*'s cabin. It was now nearly ten at night and this was my first chance to make a mug of tea and cook (reheat a takeaway curry left over from lunch) and, most important of all, as far as Stanley was concerned, was to feed him! Utilising the newly installed large table I sat down to eat and relax for the first time that day.

We had a good night's sleep on the boat and were up early for our morning walk. I filled up the fuel tank from the now open forecourt pumps and had a chat to the lady in the garage. It was still early and the bridges were not operating so I did a few little jobs (there is always something to do on a boat). I had breakfast and, before I knew it, eight o'clock had arrived and the first boat of the day was heading towards the now-open Hempsted Bridge, as the boat drew nearer I recognised it as the boat with the picture of the three cats painted on the side that we met in the Upper Lode Lock (it's a small world out there on the Cut). As the stern passed I wave hello and said, 'I'll follow you through the bridge to save it having to open twice', the guy responded helpfully by saying, 'Don't rush, I'll slow down for you'!

I cast off, then followed "Three Cats Boat" towards Gloucester. As we drew near to the city, Three Cats Boat peeled off to left to moor and I continued under Llanthony Bridge and into the Docks. Gloucester Docks Basin was very busy and full of boats but luckily there were still a couple of places left to moor on the west quay near to the lock. Once I had tied up, Stanley jumped out of *Akita* and made himself at home on the dockside in the shade of *Akita*'s roof. I put the kettle on and settled down to wait for Cat and Caroline to arrive.

Moored at Gloucester Docks

While I was waiting I decided to put my newly acquired collapsible sack truck to work. I had purchased the truck from the internet, it was advertised as being able to cope with 90 kg of weight, which would be more than enough. I carried a 25-litre jerrycan along with the truck to the water point by the Gloucester Lock. While the container was filling I erected the sack truck then lifted the now full jerrycan onto it for the return trip back to the boat. 25 litres of water weighs approximately 25 kg and the truck was meant to be able to handle 90 kg! However, as I pulled the truck loaded with only 25 kg it got harder to haul – by the time I had covered the thirty or so metres back to the boat I was dragging the thing, I felt like I was in training for a tug of war team! The wheels had splayed inwards and the poor truck looked like it had rickets! Not a good investment and it looked like I would have to continue getting longer arms and shorter legs as I was back to carrying the containers.

As is a lady's prerogative, Cat and Caroline were late getting to the docks but it was a nice sunny day and there was a myriad of boats arriving and departing, so there was plenty to hold my attention and prevent me from getting bored.

A rather grand boat arrived and expertly moored between the lock and the stern of *Akita*. There was a nice couple on board. It turned out that the gentleman was called Mike (I am not good with names or faces but given that my name is also Mike there was a fair chance that I was going to remember the name if not the face). It turn out that Mike was a member of the Gloucester Yacht Club, he was on duty in the clubhouse that night and said that we were very welcome to turn up to the club anytime. I must have looked a bit dubious but Mike assured me that the club was very informal and he truly was welcoming, I really should check it out sometime!

Cat arrived with Caroline in tow, so I called the lock on the radio and was informed that there would be a long wait due to the amount of boats that were waiting to lock down onto the River Severn. This left us with little choice than to put the kettle on and wait! After an hour I called the lock again and was informed that we could go straight into the lock, so we cast off and found that we were the only boat in the lock; I think we had been forgotten in the earlier rush.

We cruised out onto the river and as soon as we had passed the Upper Parting Cat and Caroline took turns at the wheel while I sat on the foredeck. There was a lot of debris being brought downstream, presumably washed into the river by the storms of the preceding night. As I sat there I saw a very large, half-submerged wooden fence rapidly approaching *Akita*'s bow. It was far too late to turn our boat away from it so I ran through the cabin of the boat like a greyhound after a rabbit and as soon as I reached the helm I reached out and killed the engine. The whole time I could hear the solid bulk of the wooden fence clattering down the underside of *Akita*'s hull. There was a final bang as the fence hit the outdrive leg of the quiescent motor and the three of us peered over the stern as the large wooden object appeared from under the boat.

As *Akita* drifted out of control on the river, Cat and I ripped the cushions from the seat that forms the engine cover, lifted the hatch, and squinted through the water in an attempt to examine the propeller. There was a large elongated piece of wood that was half wrapped around the outdrive leg. Cat took the wheel and did her best to steer without any propulsion, while I used the boathook to free the wood from the engine, after a few attempts it floated free to join the rest of the fence on its journey towards the south.

For the most part we were still out of control and we were drifting towards the overhanging trees on the west bank. I couldn't see the propeller but I had a quick dig around the area in its vicinity with the boathook to see if there was anything trapped there. I couldn't feel anything but in any case we were out of time. We would have to start the engine and get away from the bank before I could investigate any further. I started the engine and, hoping that the prop was still attached and in one piece, I selected forward gear.

Good old *Akita* responded. I gently took her to the centre of the river and killed the engine then, as Cat took what little control we had without the engine running, I again checked the prop. All seemed to be in order so we started up again and continued up-river listening carefully to the sound of the engine.

Yet more lessons learnt: 1. Keep a good look out for debris. 2. Have a plan in place if you do hit something. 3. Make sure you are able to inspect the propeller (make sure you take the key out of the ignition!)

No Room at the Inn

Gaining confidence that no damage had occurred, we continued towards Haw Bridge Inn where we planned to have lunch, but alas our plans were thwarted. The moorings at Haw Bridge were fully occupied – there was literally no room at the Inn! The thought did cross my mind that I could "breast up" (moor up to another boat) but I was not sure what the etiquette for doing this was – I didn't know the owners of the long narrowboat currently residing at the pontoon so I decided to turn around and head back down-river to The Boat Inn at Ashleworth Quay. We were all starting to get hungry now and it was another forty minutes or so before we arrived at The Boat Inn only to find out they were not serving food! Cat made us a quick snack while I topped up the fuel tank and we head back to Gloucester Docks.

A short time later *Akita* arrived back at the Upper Parting and, as is protocol, I called Gloucester Lock on the radio, there was no response so after repeated attempts both on the phone and on the radio I reduced *Akita*'s speed to tick-over so we were barely making any headway and kept trying to call the lock. Because I could not contact the lock, I didn't know if there were any large vessels heading up the river towards us so we were all keeping a good look out forward. I also did not want to arrive at the lock unannounced. A long time later, almost as we had the lock in sight, the keeper responded on the radio and informed me that I would have to tie up to the chains well before the lock and wait. This was a first for me but really was quite easy to do. I brought *Akita* in close to the wall selected reverse and once we were at a stop simply fed a stern line through the chain, tied off, then let *Akita* slowly drift forward with the current until the rope held, Cat then secured the bow and we settled down to wait. (Note: You normally moor facing into the current on a river, however, *do not* attempt to turn around and do so before Gloucester Lock, you should tie up stern first and facing the lock!)

Due to the long wait for the lock on the outbound leg of our journey and coupled with this delay for the lock on the way back and the very restrictive opens hours of the G&S bridges, I was resigned to the fact that we were not going to make it back to our home mooring for the night. It was fortunate that this was Saturday and not a Sunday or I would have been in trouble because I would not have been able to move the boat again until the next weekend. The more time I spent on the boat, the more the restrictive opening hours on the Gloucester & Sharpness Canal became a problem. If this had been a Sunday I would have had to leave *Akita* out on the canal unattended for the working week. Surely there must be a better way of running the canal? The simple solution would to have the bridges and locks manned until half an hour after last light throughout the year – this would allow you to make the maximum use of the daylight hours to cruise.

Once the lock was ready we locked up into the basin. There was only one space left to moor and this was on one of the finger pontoons. The wind was gusting across the docks and I knew that it would be "fun" trying to moor, but I was resolved to try and accepted that it would take a few attempts to get into the space; in the end it took four tries.

Even though the hordes of people in the docks were watching my attempts to moor, I had not been stressed, which surprised me, but once *Akita* was safely tied up I sat down and thought about the reason for my lack of anxiety. It was simple; the key was "acceptance"; I knew that the wind would push *Akita* away from my intended course and I knew and accepted that it would take a few attempts to dock, so that was it, acceptance was the way forward! The other boaters seem to already know this because none of them were giving me funny or sceptical looks and one even commented on how hard it was to get into the mooring in the gusting wind. So there was another lesson learnt: you have to accept that things are not always going to go your way and you will have to be prepared to persevere.

The consolation for being stuck in the docks was that I could have a good curry from Vinings Restaurant, which was consumed on board the boat and we were getting comfortable. However, both Cat and I agreed that we did not want to spend another sleep-deprived night aboard *Akita* on a noisy Saturday evening in the docks. Cat departed in a taxi to fetch her car in order to transport Stanley, Caroline, and me home.

Just as Cat returned with the car, a large fireworks display started up – poor Stanley was extremely stressed and was shaking with terror. I tried to impart to him the "acceptance" lesson but he did not seem to appreciate the sentiment and needed no encouragement to jump into the back of the car. If he could have driven he would have wheel-spun out of the car park.

Early the following morning, after bidding farewell to Caroline, we returned to *Akita* and we were the first boat of the morning to pass under Llanthony Bridge. As we approached Hempsted Bridge no traffic lights were displayed, this was very odd! The only thing I could think of was that the bridge was unmanned; this was then confirmed by someone shouting from the towpath. The bridge has an air draft of only 1.4 metres so we were going nowhere and were left with no option other than to moor. I called back to Gloucester Lock on the radio and was informed that someone had failed to show up for work but that a replacement keeper was on his way from another bridge to assist and would be with us in ten minutes – more than enough time to make a mug of tea! The stand in keep turned up in good time and we were soon on our way. It had started to rain but we were nice and dry under the pram cover roof. However, we could have done with windscreen wipers! As we were making our final approach to moor at our pontoon the dreaded weeds in the marina wrapped themselves around the prop once again; luckily we were lined up quite well and just drifted into our mooring, unluckily we were unable to stop and "bumped" into Mark's boat before coming to a rest with a thud against the pontoon, I was so pleased that I had just added a second bow fender!

Sunday was rapidly drawing to a close and it was time once again to secure *Akita* for the working week.

Security Matters

When we first acquired our boat, one of the reasons for its sad state of disrepair was that it had previously been vandalised and the subsequent repair and refurbishment had been botched. I do not think I will ever know the reason that compelled the person or persons to damage the boat or if they had any reason at all. But even though the incident happened long before we even thought about buying a boat, it has affected our thinking about security.

We never leave anything of value on board *Akita* – it is a simple matter of putting the regular items into a bag to take with us when we leave the boat: the VHF radio, mobile phones, wallets, and cameras, etc., always go with us, after that there is little of any monetary value left aboard. We always try to remember to close all the blinds so a would-be thief cannot see into the cabin; and we always close and lock the doors. Sometimes I will leave some music playing loud enough so that it can be heard just outside the boat, I hope that this will dissuade crooks from trying to enter by making them think that someone is aboard. We are also quite careful where we leave our boat; sometime we just get the "wrong vibe" about a place and so we move on.

Also, there is rather big dog that resides on our boat so you never know if Stanley is lying in wait to "entertain" an uninvited "guest", he does so like a bit of company and never seems to have enough chew toys!

Once you get to know other boaters in your area you soon realise that they will keep an eye on your boat and you in turn will reciprocate the favour. If it is true what they say that some people who dwell in houses no longer talk to, or sometime don't even know the names of their neighbours, the same does not appear to be the case for the boating community, where old-fashioned neighbourly values seem to be the norm! I am not saying that there is a breakdown in neighbourly behaviour in the housing estates throughout this land of ours but that is what I am told, and this made me wonder why this would be the case?

I think that perhaps that in no small part it is to do with having something in common with your neighbour. Not so very long ago; people living on housing estates, terraced houses, or in other communities would quite often have in common the fact that they would all work in the same industry or even for the same employer, but the larger, heavy industries, like the mines, steel, and car manufacturers being grouped in one geographical location are now gone. People living next door or across the road from each other no longer have this, or it seems much of anything else, in common; one person maybe an I.T. consultant and their neighbour could well be a doctor, dentist, or HGV driver. Whereas if you live on or spend a lot of time on a boat the very fact that you are on a vessel is enough to give you plenty in common with your fellow boater; and once you get talking to them, you quite often find you have other things in common too! Perhaps the doctor or dentist should try talking to their HGV driver neighbour, they might find they have more in common than they think, after all we should not defined by our jobs!

Canal Time

We had owned the boat for months now; and to date I had only half-heartedly attempted to lift the engine, however, due to our problems with wood and weeds on the propeller it now seemed prudent to see how to lift the inboard/outboard engine so that I could inspect the prop. This proved to be quite easy in fact. Simply push down on a lever and then lift and tilt the engine backwards on its mounting, then latch into place with another lever. The only things that would slow the process were that the seat/engine cover had to be lifted and a hatch in the transom (back of the boat) also had to be opened. I practised this a few times until I was proficient with the procedure; this gave me confidence that I could inspect/clear the prop in the event of future incidents without blindly poking around with the boathook. Now that I could see the propeller, it was obvious even to me that it would need to be replaced; it was probable that it was the original prop, and the poor thing looked like it had hit everything possible in its twenty-five years of service, from bricks and shopping trolleys to wayward submarines. It was disfigured, bent out of shape, and there were chunks missing from the blades; it would have to be retired.

The weekend was drawing to a close and it was time to once again face up to the grim reality that I am not a man of independent wealth. The only problem with weekends is that they have to end!

While weekends have to end they also have to start

again; Friday evening saw me walking Stanley before driving to the marina, this was done in order avoid a repeat of Stanley's not-so-little accident in the back of the van the previous weekend. Cat was already on the boat and had dinner ready and waiting for me (what a girl!). We then took Stanley on our normal walk circumnavigating the marina before settling down for the night. The walk was repeated the following morning and then Cat drove to Bristol to visit her mum for the day.

I was meant to get an early start and take the boat to Gloucester to get a new propeller, however, Mark returned from a long night out and we got talking, each of us sitting on the decks of our respective boats. It was after nine and the bridges had been open for over an hour before I cast off, it was nice not to have to rush about for once – as Gary, whose boat also resides in the marina would say, I was 'on Canal Time, no need to rush!'

I cruised to Gloucester but was unable to obtain a new prop although I was advised where I could source one, but there was no way that would happen today! The fact that the prop could not be replaced that day was a bit worrying because Cat and I were planning a long cruise in two weeks' time, and the prop would have to be replaced before the voyage. I would have to remove the prop and take it to a supplier next Saturday – this would only leave a few days for them to obtain one for me.

As I was already near the local supermarket, I decided to do some food shopping. I was in and out of the shop in lightning-quick time and loaded the food into *Akita*. I had just left the mooring outside the supermarket when I could see a boat coming the other way. This boat had far too many people on the roof and was zigzagging all over the canal; this could only mean one thing – a hire boat!

Hire boats should be avoided and if they are "crewed" by a party of drunk blokes and the one who is steering is wearing a Ship's Captain hat, is supporting himself on the tiller, and has a bottle of booze in his hand, this is doubly true. As we passed each other the occupants of the happy boat waved and pointed at Stanley and I waved back giving their out of control vessel a very wide berth. I know it is wrong but they did look funny, and did seem to be having fun. They crashed into the mooring outside the supermarket, half-jumped, half-fell onto the quay, and then went to "refuel" from the shop's wine, spirits, and beer department. It looked like they were having a great time and it was still only midday!

I stopped off to refuel (with petrol not booze), and it was here that I had a lucky escape. I tied Stanley's lead around the single pole that supports the driver seat and then allowed him to jump out of the boat and lie on the pontoon as he likes to do. I then carried the fuel tank to the garage to fill. When I returned I replaced the tank and only then did I realise what I had done. It is all very well tying your dog to the seat post but this is no good whatsoever if you then stupidly lift the seat out of its mounting to make it easier to get out of the boat, leaving the lead lying on the deck not tied to anything! Luckily for me Stanley did not realise that he could run free and did not make a break for freedom and the main road. The first job that I did on my return to the marina was to put in a strong point to hitch Stanley up to that was within easy reach of the driver position.

Still being on "Canal Time" I was not in a rush to get back to the marina so I stopped just after Parkend Bridge to let Stanley stretch his legs. We walked back along the Cut chatting to other boaters as we went. As we were returning to *Akita* I could hear a noise coming from back down the canal, the clamour was emanating from HMS *Bargain Booze* as she weaved her drunken way back along the canal – it was just as well it was a wide ship canal or they would have crashed into the side! Not wanting to join the party I hastily pulled up the mooring stakes and made off down the Cut.

Once the strong point to hitch Stanley had been installed, I was surprised by how late in the day it was (real time does not seem to appreciate the concept of Canal Time). It was already mid-evening, Cat had returned with an Indian takeaway, and after we had eaten it was time for Stanley's final walk of the day.

During my cruising up and down the G&S I had noticed some work being carried out on some new canalside moorings just north of Parkend Bridge near to a white building called The Castle; there were electric and water points being installed. I decided to look into the possibility of getting a berth there – if this were possible then the stress of getting to the marina and then getting past the first two bridges on a Friday night would not apply (we would already be north of the two low bridges). True, we still would not get all the way to Gloucester and the River Severn before the other low bridges had closed, but we could never make this anyway.

We jumped into the campervan on the Sunday morning and drove from the marina so that Cat could have a look. After seeing our potential new mooring, which was still very much a work in progress, she did not seem to be put off by the prospect of moving, so it was agreed that I would make some more enquires during the following week. If we could move, I would miss some of the people in the marina, but moving would help in a small way to negate the problems caused by the crazy opening hours of the G&S bridges.

We decided to install a new counter above Stanley's "Bed" – this meant having to drive home and collect tools and wood and then return to start work. While I was doing this Cat would go shopping and then get some food together for the worker (me). A new large counter was duly installed giving us both a feeling that with each little improvement we made to *Akita* living aboard got that little bit easier.

There are a few different types of toilets available for use on boats that cruise the inland waterways: the main two types are pump out and cassette (porta-potty). We use a porta-potty; the waste is collected in a detachable cassette, once the cassette is full (or preferably before) you then carry it to a disposal site (Elsan disposal point) and empty it out, this really is not as bad as it sounds! The advantage of this type of loo is that it is normally free to empty; the disadvantage is that the cassette capacity is not that great so you do have to empty it when you get the chance. We have a spare cassette stored away in the boat but to date we have never had to use it!

Akita was also fitted with a pump out system but the toilet was removed before we owned the vessel. The advantage of a pump out system is that you have a large capacity storage tank so can you go for longer before having to empty (or pump out) the tank. The disadvantage is that there is a cost involved to pump out and in any event you really should carry a spare porta-potty just in case you are unable to find a pump out station.

One of the major jobs that I had been putting off was the removal of the redundant "black water" or "pump out" tank; this is the tank that collected the human waste from the old toilet (you can see why I was procrastinating!) Previously I had looked at doing it but I couldn't see how I would get it out from its cavity through the small doors that were enclosing it. Now I had a bit of free time and, with closer inspection, I could see that there were only four screws holding the door frame in place; once the frame was removed it was just a case of disconnecting the pipes and then manhandling the large tank out, hoping that none of the contents would spill. Both Cat and I pulled, lifted and pushed the large tank and deposited it into our campervan. Once the tank was out of the boat we had a whole lot more storage space; it turned out to be a most productive weekend and all done in Canal Time!

Waste Water, Wonder, and Wanderlust

One of the things that intrigued me before we had a boat was where did the liquid waste go? Surely it would not go straight into the canal!

It is quite rightly illegal to allow human waste to drain into the UK's inland waterway system (the G&S Canal is part of Bristol's water supply) hence the toilet systems mentioned previously. However, at the time of writing, water from your sink and shower is allowed to drain directly into the Cut. Pull the plug in your sink and if you have a window open you will hear the water pouring into the canal. I know it is sad, but the kid in me still likes to hear the water pouring into the Cut, sometimes I will pull the plug and then stick my head out of the window to see the water escaping out of the side of the boat. Given the fact that that waste water does go straight into the waterway; consideration should be given to the type of washing-up liquid, soap, and shampoo being used on board a boat, eco-friendly products are available and perhaps should be considered.

The working week arrived and it was time to enquire about the potential new mooring – a phone call or two later and *Akita* was on the end of a very long waiting list, so long in fact that we would be moving sometime in the next decade or so. I was very disappointed because we would still be trapped by the bridges and their unaccommodating opening times, but I was also happy because both Cat and I felt at home in the marina.

However comfortable we felt in the marina, it was just not practical to stay there long-term if we wanted to use the canal to cruise during the long summer evenings or get a head start on a Friday evening for a weekend cruise on the River Severn, something would have to give! I was still hoping that the bridge opening times would be changed to more practical and user-friendly hours, everyone I spoke to seemed to be in agreement, something had to change!

Prior Preparation Prevents ...

It was now mid-August and a bank holiday was rapidly approaching; Cat had just started a new job, but both she and I had booked a day or two either side of the bank holiday off work so we would have five days to cruise. We were planning to go up the River Severn and then get on to the Worcester & Birmingham Canal, or maybe continue on up north and give the recently reopened Droitwich Barge Canal a go, or even go all the way to Stourport on Severn; it was nice to be flexible.

I was really looking forward to the trip – it would be our first multiple-night cruise away from our home mooring. There was only one weekend to go before our trip so I was planning to do one or two jobs on *Akita* and then give her a good check-over ready for our holiday, but the most important thing to do was to replace the battered propeller!

The maintenance weekend arrived, so on Friday evening I could be seen hanging off the back of the boat trying to remove the propeller with one hand while hanging on with the other, this was not working! To free up my other hand I use Stanley's lead to tie myself to the back of the boat – I was perched precariously on a small fold-down step on the stern of *Akita* and was now able to work on the prop. It proved very easy to detach. The split-pin was removed, then the castle nut, next the spacer, and then the propeller was slid off the drive shaft spine. Very easy and I didn't drop anything into the water. It was going too well, surely something would go wrong!

First thing Saturday morning I drove the twenty minutes to the marine suppliers, and after lots of scraping and cleaning the much-worn number on the propeller was just about legible. The new prop was ordered and would be ready to be picked up in a few days' time. Things were still going well, this was too good to be true!

With the holiday approaching, I was aware that because we would be away from the marina and the electrical hook-up we would only be able to run our 12-volt fridge while the engine was running, otherwise we would soon drain the battery that powered our lights and water pump. To combat this problem I spent some time installing a second leisure battery and another split charger; the idea being that we would only use this battery for the fridge should we wish to use the fridge when the engine was not running, in the event that we ran this battery down it would not affect the starter or main leisure batteries.

Ever since we had had the boat; there was on board a very old empty jerrycan that looked like it had seen service in the Second World War (and possibly the Boer War). It had been abandoned by the previous owner – the lid would not close and to date we had just been using it as a foot-rest when sitting on the driver's seat, I now decided that it had to go! Cannibalising an old step I made a foot-rest and now at last we had one of the correct size and we could store some kit under it. But the best thing was that we could finally get rid of the old battered jerrycan, perhaps the Imperial War Museum would like it?

The bed on the boat proved to be very spacious and comfortable, but when it was not being used there was not really anywhere to store the boards that made up the centre of the bed. A week or so previously I had installed a counter above Stanley's bed and I had come up with the idea of putting a shelf just underneath this counter for the bed boards to be stored on. This job did not take long, and now it is finished the boards can be stored out of sight, out of the way, and they are easily accessible.

The whole summer had been great so far and it was another very sunny day. Stanley needed a walk so I took him to the Canal Heritage Centre fifteen minutes' walk from our mooring, I bought a wall map of the inland waterways; I thought it would look good mounted on the wall in *Akita*. While on our walk I saw another boat which looked very similar to *Akita* – it was only the second boat I had seen that in any way resembled ours. I wanted to shout across to the figures standing on the stern deck to tell them I had the same boat, but I knew they would not be able to hear me over the noise of their engine and would probably think that I was nuts! The rest of weekend was spent clearing out and sorting the cupboards and topping up the water tanks ready for a quick getting away the following Thursday evening.

Monday and work once again intruded. I called the marine suppliers to make sure they had ordered the propeller, not good news! They had tried to order the prop only to be told that there was no chance of getting one for two months – that was no good to me, we needed one in three days' time! The marine suppliers said that they would try to get a second-hand or refurbished prop and I should call back after lunch …

Ever the pessimist (realist) I called the suppliers as agreed and waited for them to deliver the bad news. To my surprise they had managed to find a second-hand prop which they assured me, 'looks like new'. In fact I was reliably informed that: 'it looks like it was a display model that had been left on the shelf'. This was great news – all that was required now was for my mum to pick it up for me (I was stuck at work) and then for me to fit it the first evening that I could, but for now all I could do was just hope that it fitted.

So that we do not forget anything, Cat and I have

system in place, we call this the "to go box". It really is very simple, the box has its own place in the boat, anything that needs to go home is placed into it throughout our time aboard, and then at the end of the trip the box is taken home. Likewise the to go box has its own place in the front porch of our house – anything that needs to go back to the boat is placed into it throughout the week. This simple system works fine, as long as you remember to take the to go box!

While looking at the BBC news website I came across an article about a 36-foot cruiser that had caught fire on the River Ouse. The couple on board managed to escape and were rescued but the vessel was burnt out and sank, and as a safety precaution the river had to be closed to all shipping. As I watched the video of the inferno I tried to imagine how the unfortunate pair felt, and how Cat and I (and Stanley) would react if this had been *Akita*. There was already a fire blanket and two fire extinguishers on board *Akita*, but after seeing the video of the gutted hull finally sinking below the waves I put another extinguisher into the to go box – I would not want to see *Akita* die that way.

During Wednesday I received a phone call from Mum to inform me that she had collected the "newish" propeller, and that she was going to leave it on the deck of the boat for me. I was stuck at work, and still could only hope that it was the correct type and that it would fit. At the end of the working day I rushed home, took Stanley for his walk then shot down to the marina. There, sitting on the deck, was a cardboard box containing the prop. I opened it and compared the new propeller with the old, they looked comparable – so far, so good!

Once again I tied myself to the boat and after removing everything from my pockets just in case I fell into the water, I stepped onto the small fold-down step at the stern of *Akita* and started to fit the new propeller. All went well and nothing was dropped into the water. The hardest part was putting the split pin in place through the hole in the nut and shaft, but after a bit of messing about even this was achieved and the job was complete, I remained dry and we once again had a vessel with propulsion.

Everything that we wanted on our trip was in the van and I loaded it into *Akita* ready for the cruise. I now had one last job to complete then I could go home and get some sleep. The original pump-out toilet had been removed before we had the boat, but there was a large cube-shaped block of wood that it had once sat on. Our porta-potty sat on the shower tray and it was a bit low when you were sitting on it and, because of the surround at the base of the shower tray, it was difficult to stand up once your "mission" was complete. This was not a problem if you only use the loo one or twice but if you are using it over the course of a long weekend it becomes tedious. I installed a wooden platform on top of the old pump-out toilet block to mount our porta-potty on; this freed up the shower tray, tidied up the area around the location of the old pump-out throne and raised the porta-potty to a more comfortable height – not bad for a Wednesday evening's work. Time for bed!

Thursday and the day of the getaway arrived but first I would have to spend the day at work. We were having some renovations done to the house and the workmen were due to start work at the rear of the property. As good builders are hard to find and I did not want to return home to find severed limbs all over the back garden, I had to take Stanley to work with me. He spent the day in the shade of the campervan and I had to nip out and take him for little walks throughout the day. I didn't like leaving him there but I was left with little choice. I should not have worried – he made himself at home and was made a fuss of by everyone who passed by.

One advantage of having Stanley with me was that at the end of the day I could drive straight from the office to

133

the marina, this would save time and assist me in my effort to get past the first two bridges. The plan was for Cat to visit her mum straight after she finished work on Thursday evening while I cruised *Akita* as close to Gloucester as I could. Cat would then do some shopping at the supermarket near to Gloucester Docks early on Friday morning, while I brought the boat up and moored outside the shop ready to pick her up. We would then try to lock down onto the River Severn as early as we could, thus avoiding the tide that we had been informed would possibly be bringing a lot of debris on to the navigable part of the river, and we really did not want to hit any more fences!

The Getaway Starts with a Splash

The working day came to an end, and, after taking Stanley for a wee walk, we jumped in to the van and headed off to pick up the boat. All of our gear was already aboard so I did a quick check over everything and we headed north on the G&S. Once again we just made it past the low bridges before they closed.

As soon as we were past the Parkend swing bridge, I headed to the bank to moor so that Stanley could have a proper walk. I pulled alongside and told Stanley to wait as I reached over to pick up the mooring stake and hammer. From behind me I heard Stanley's claws on the side of the boat as he started to exit. 'WAIT!' I shouted to him but he had already made a leap for the grassy bank, and unfortunately he didn't make it.

I rushed across the deck and peered over the side to see poor Stanley splashing about in the decreasing gap between boat and bank. Stanley was trying to claw his way up the vertical steel pylons that lined the side of the canal but the water was over two foot lower than the bank and there was no way he could make it. All I could do was hold the boat away from the side so that he wasn't crushed between the bank and the hull while keeping hold of his lead to try to keep him afloat.

As all this was happening I picked up movement from my peripheral vision, it turned out to be a man on a mountain bike riding along the towpath. I knew that

Stanley was now in real trouble and did not hesitate in shouting out for help. The guy on the bike was great and stopped to assist – he tried to pull Stanley out, but Stan weighs over 52 kg dry and he was now very wet, so there was no way one man could lift him on his own, and I was still stuck on board holding the boat away to stop it from crushing Stanley. The guy was making a valiant attempt to pull Stanley out but he was never going to succeed and, as he pulled, the buckle on Stan's harness broke and the guy had to let go. Poor Stanley now turned around, headed back to the boat and tried to claw his way up the side. I was still holding his lead to keep his head above water but now his harness was broken, and for the first time Stan's head went under the water. As I looked in to his eyes I could tell that he knew he was in real trouble. We had to have a rethink and come up with a plan fast.

I threw the mooring stake and hammer to the man on the bank, not being a boater he hammered the stake into the ground so far that I thought he was trying to impale someone in Australia. He quickly secured the boat to the inch of mooring stake that still protruded above the ground. I jumped ashore as the guy stopped Stanley from sinking by holding on to the loose fur around his chin. Having no other option, the man was basically holding Stan by the throat and he said to me, 'Do you think he'll bite me?' However, Stanley must have known that this total stranger was trying to help, because as the guy held him Stanley licked his forearms, as he did this I thought the guy was going to break down in tears – it was such nice moment in the middle of all the stress.

We both lay on the bank, reaching down towards Stanley. I gathered the chest strap of the harness and held it together at the point where it had broken and then on the count of three, the guy and I lifted Stanley up. As soon as Stan's paws were on top of the bank he assisted with his own rescue. As the three of us stood on the side of the canal, Stanley thanked us by doing what dogs invariably do, and shook the water from his coat. I did ask the man's name but with the drama and the fact that I am useless with names I forgot it – so if it was you who helped Stanley and me out, thank you very much!

Thankfully it was yet another sunny day and Stanley was well on the way to drying out by the time we got back to *Akita*. He did not seem to be shaken up after his dip in the G&S Canal, and he just jumped back onboard as if nothing had happened!

We cruised up to the now-closed Hempstead Bridge and then settled down for the night to wait for the bridges to start operating in the morning.

Friday morning dawned and I topped up the fuel tank (I always go onto the river with a full tank). As soon as I could pass through the bridge I met up with Cat outside the supermarket. We had learnt our lesson and were buying everything before our cruise. Once *Akita*'s larder was fully stocked we joined four other boats in Gloucester Lock ready to be lowered down onto the River Severn. While we were locking down I had the chance to chat to the skipper of a very nice cruiser that we was alongside, it turned out that he used to have a boat very similar to *Akita* and gave me some useful information about our craft.

Once the gates were opened the narrowboats departed, followed by the cruiser, and *Akita* brought up the rear. We followed the winding river towards the north, as the last of the narrowboats cleared the Upper Parting and emerged onto the wider part of the Severn, the cruiser used its superior speed to overtake the line of steel-hulled boats.

Taking it in turns to steer, Cat and I cruised up the Severn against the current as far as Haw Bridge. We stopped and tied up to the good moorings so that Stanley could have a little walk. We were only gone for fifteen minutes but when we returned the river was flowing in the opposite direction – it was a stark reminder that the River

Severn is tidal, even this far up-river. A small cruiser had been moored facing up-river but had only been secured from the bow; it had been pushed away from its mooring and was sideways across the river and being held against another boat by the inverted flow of the water. There was another lesson – albeit an obvious one, always secure your bow and stern!

We left our mooring and were making good time going up-river on the water that was continuing to flow towards the north and away from the sea, but all good things come to an end and the tide started to ebb as we approached Upper Lode Lock. Once through the lock the river is pretty much non-tidal so we continued north once more against the flow of the river.

The visitor moorings at Upton-upon-Severn were predictably very busy and there was not a space left. One of the main problems with the River Severn is that there are not enough good moorings along its length. This, coupled with the fact that the locks close at a ridiculously early time, means you have to plan well ahead and make sure you find a safe mooring for the night. We pulled in to Upton Marina and were lucky to get one of the last places on this busy bank holiday weekend.

For such a small place there always seems to be something happening at Upton – last time I was here there was a folk festival taking place, this weekend there was a music festival with many bands popular in the seventies and eighties on the bill. It seemed these bands still had a following because the large field on the east side of the river was filling up with tents and campervans while a steady procession of vehicles were queuing to get onto the site.

Upton seems like a nice place to visit with loads of pubs and restaurants, some river-side, others away from the water, and happily for me there is a curry house! We had a walk around the small town and once a takeaway curry had been obtained we headed back to *Akita* to eat. Because the marina was not far from the festival field we could occasionally hear the sound of the festival as it was carried on the wind towards us, which was nearly as good as being there.

Stanley enjoying the view on the G&S Canal

The next morning we were up early and after taking Stanley for his walk headed back out onto the river to make the most of the day's cruising. We left Upton and some two hours or so later we arrived at the double locks at Diglis.

Diglis locks are set side by side and the traffic lights were displaying a green arrow, directing us into the smaller lock on the east side of the river. We departed from the lock, waving our thanks to the keeper, and within a few minutes we were again mooring up on the east bank of the Severn in the centre of Worcester.

You know how things seem smaller now that you are an adult than they did when you were a kid? That was exactly how I now felt – the river seemed narrower than it did when I first cruised through Worcester on my maiden voyage home. The part of Worcester lining the river seemed shorter and I was not bothered by the amount of craft cruising around. Even the steps leading up the banks at the side of the river seemed not so steep. My whole perspective had changed; I felt at home in *Akita*, I felt in control of my boat, and even on this busy part of the river I felt relaxed. The only way I can describe it is that when I had first stepped onboard our new boat some five months or so before, I had been an adolescent who knew it all in theory but really knew nothing at all in practice. In fact everything seemed big, strange, and confusing. But now I was growing up; I was not so overawed by situations, and I was seeing things for what they were.

Remembering the café from my trip down-river early in the year, I led Cat and Stanley up the steps towards the Severn Café and an all-day breakfast. I can wholeheartedly recommend the café to all who may be passing; the staff made us feel very welcome – they even produced a bowl of water for Stanley, the food was just right, and it is only a minute or so from the moorings.

Feeling somewhat bloated due to our all-day breakfast, we resumed our cruise north. Cat was at the helm so I phoned ahead to see if I could book us a spot for the night at the Stourport Marina. We were allocated a mooring on the "Hammerhead" (T-shaped mooring at the end of the pontoon), and as this was the same spot that Dave and I had stopped at on our first trip home, I knew just where to go. Once *Akita* was secured, the three of us walked to the marina office to pay for our night's mooring (very reasonable price). We then walked along the side of the river and into Stourport town in search of a curry. It was still early so we stopped to watch hire-boat crews working the narrow canal locks as they made their way from the river and on to the Staffordshire & Worcestershire Canal. Cat and I had decided to take a short cruise along the newly reopened Droitwich Barge Canal on our way home. Cat had still not seen or operated manual canal locks so being able to now see some locks being operated proved to be very useful.

One thing that did worry me was the fact that some of the "crews" were made up of youngsters that were really too young to be working the locks. Locks can be dangerous places with unprotected long drops, deep turbulent water, and heavy boats drifting about in them. Working the paddles can be hard work. I watched a young girl of about thirteen struggling to wind up the heavy paddles while her long hair was on the verge of getting caught up in the gear mechanism. She then stopped trying to wind up the paddles and, while barely holding onto the windlass with one hand, started to complain about the grease that she had got on her other hand, while prodding the exposed gears with her fingers. I did not want to say anything to the parents, but this was a recipe for disaster and I was relieved when an adult finally took over. If the girl had let go of the windlass it would have spun out of control and could have broken her arm or worse! Not wishing to loiter around the potential scene of carnage, we wandered off to acquire a takeaway and then made our way back to *Akita* to round off Saturday evening with a curry.

Learning Lock Lessons on the Droitwich Barge Canal

Early Sunday morning we cruised back down-river, then turned east and moored up to the pontoon before the first lock on the Droitwich Barge Canal. The first few locks are wide and capable of admitting a barge or two narrowboats side by side. It felt strange to be responsible for working the locks once again after spending so much time on the river where the locks are all operated by keepers. This would be the first time that Cat and I had operated the locks together as a team and we would have to find a system that would work for us.

Leaving *Akita* with Stanley safely aboard we walked up to the lock to have a look. It was full of water and set against us. I despatched Cat to go forward to see if there were any boats coming the other way that could use the lock as it was set, and dug out the long-lost windlasses ready to work the lock paddles, then walked back up to the lock to hear Cat's report

No boats were inbound, so I wound the heavy paddles to release the water in the lock chamber, and *Akita* moved around on her rope in the now turbulent water. Once the lock was empty we started to open the large weighty gates – I found it difficult to get my gate moving and poor Cat, who was still not fully recovered from her operation, could not get hers moving at all, and had to accept help from some kindly passers by.

It became apparent that we would have to modify our approach to operating the locks. At least until Cat was fully recovered and fitter, she would have to steer our boat in and out of the locks and I would work all the paddles and gates. Cat expressed her misgivings about controlling the boat in the locks but she took up the challenge and controlled the boat well enough to avoid any damage (don't tell her, but I think she did better than I did in my first few locks).

We worked our way through the first two locks, then with Cat at the helm cruised eastwards along the Droitwich Barge Canal. The navigation was very narrow due to the fact that it was hemmed in on both sides by very tall reeds, so tall in fact that you could not see further than a few feet ahead of the bow. I went forward and stood on the roof to give Cat warning of oncoming vessels, but even with me in this elevated position we did not get much forewarning when we met the first boat heading in the opposite direction. Cat (and the other boater) did well to avoid each other and we passed without incident.

Cat's confidence was growing so much that she allowed Stanley and me to disembark and run along the towpath ahead of *Akita*. This was good for two reasons: I could warn her about oncoming boats and Stanley was getting a good workout. We would run for twenty or so metres then there would be a break cut in to in the wall of reeds and Stanley would stop and peer though the gap to wait for Cat to appear (he is such a Mummy's boy) then we would be off again running ahead to the next gap to repeat the process.

With our new system in place we started to work our way through Mildenham Mill Lock; a family of swans were making a lot of noise and it was not until we were halfway through the lock that I realised that they had been separated. One cygnet was at the head (upper level) on the east side of the lock, the mother was in the chamber, and while daddy remained on the bank, the remaining cygnets were on tail (the lower level of the lock). I felt guilty about any part that I may have played in their separation but there was not a lot I could do about it. As we opened the gate to exit the one cygnet could now at least make its way towards Mum.

With Stanley and me running along the towpath and Cat steering *Akita* we went as far as Ladywood Bottom Lock and there we reluctantly decided that we would have to turn around and head back towards the river. We would have liked to have kept going but we knew that time was limited and we had planned to get home with one day to spare in case there were any problems on the way; we could not be late for work!

Lock Liaisons

The canal was just wide enough for me to turn *Akita* around. As I did so I reflected that this would have been a very messy operation if I had attempted this turn three or so months before, but I could now almost spin her around on the spot with barely any forwards or backwards movement. As we were turning, or winding as we boaters say (I was finally starting to think of myself as a boater), two other narrowboats had worked their way through Ladywood Bottom Lock and would follow us westward towards the River Severn. On our arrival back at Mildenham Mill Lock, it was still set for us so I opened the gates but then waited for the other narrowboats to enter. The first boat was only 26 foot long but of steel construction and the second was about 60 foot long, also made of steel and was named *The Black Pig*. If you are going to share a lock the general rule is that the steel boats go in first and the GRP craft afterwards; this is not done for any hierarchical reasons but is purely a practical arrangement so that GRP vessels do not get damaged by the heavier and more robust steel boats. The 26-footer cruised into to the lock chamber and then the larger boat followed and stopped alongside. I then manoeuvred in behind the smaller boat. I was surprised that we all fitted in the lock with room to spare! Sharing the lock is very good practice – it saves water and the workload is halved, it is also very sociable.

We were through the lock in record time and the other two boats left to prep the next lock while I closed the gates on this one, very efficient! Cat was now back at the helm and she was waiting for me just outside the lock. I took one last glance to make sure all the gates and paddles were closed and then hopped back onboard *Akita*, Cat pushed the throttle forward, and we were off in pursuit of our fellow boaters and the next lock.

As we made our way back towards Hawford Bridge I was pleased to see that the family of swans were now safely reunited and seemed none the worse for their ordeal. We approached Hawford Top Lock to see *The Black Pig* waiting at the lock – the other smaller craft had caught up with another boat and had already locked down.

The lock was now set against us and the crew of *The Black Pig* had already worked the paddles and the chamber was refilling, this left me with a bit of spare time and I took the opportunity to top up the fuel tank so that I could once again enter the river with a full tank.

The lock was ready and the larger narrowboat was already moving into the chamber by the time I had completed refuelling *Akita*'s main tank. I steered our boat into the chamber alongside *The Black Pig* then, as Cat took over at the helm, I stepped onto the top of the lock to help with the operation of getting our two boats through. It was so much easier and very enjoyable working the locks with the other boat crew; we were very lucky to have had the opportunity to be working with a seasoned crew who knew what they were doing.

Southbound Again

We left Hawford Bottom Lock and cruised back on to the Severn and into Bevere River Lock to share it with our new friends for the last time. The large gates opened and waving goodbye to our lock buddies we cruised out and continued south toward Worcester where we moored on the river under a willow tree and conveniently close to the Severn Café.

I was confident that we would have enough petrol to get us home; however, I thought it would be prudent to stock up here as we were in back in civilisation, after all we were in a city with major roads all around us, a service station could not be that far away, could it?

With an empty fuel tank and the foldable sack truck I headed toward the road. Most people I asked for directions turned out to be tourists and did not have a clue where a filling station could be found. I did ask one local who gave me very good directions to a garage forecourt only for me to find out that they only sold cars and NO petrol! After trudging along the roads towing the truck behind me like a lost little boy looking for his mum; I finally found a filling station right next to the Worcester & Birmingham Canal (if only we had been on that canal!) I filled up the tank and sweating in the blazing sun headed back towards the river and *Akita*, it was now that I remembered the problem with the sack truck! The wheels kept splaying inwards and I had to stop every fifteen metres to kick the wheels out and back into position before dragging the damn thing onwards. It took thirty minutes to get back to the boat and by this time I was sweating and cursing in equal measure, and also very hungry.

Akita has a petrol in board/out board motor, however, the vast majority of narrowboats have engines that run on diesel which is safer, more economical, and is more widely available on the Inland Waterways Network. For the most part diesel engines are more flexible and, as well as providing propulsion, can also act as generators supplying the vessel with 240-volt electricity and hot water for washing and showering. A boat can also be heated by utilising a drip feed diesel stove, although the majority of narrowboats use a solid fuel stove that can burn coal, coke, and logs. These stoves are sometimes fitted with back boilers which can feed radiators in other parts of the boat, and in some cases hot water for washing and showering. Diesel engines can be more expensive to buy and maintain, but over all are probably a better fit for a narrowboat. Perhaps one day I'll buy a boat with diesel propulsion but for the time being we are happy with our little *Akita*.

Cat offered to go and get the curry while I had a well-deserved snooze, but as soon as I was reclining in a vain attempt to sleep, a multitude of Dragon Boats now decided that this would be a good bit of river to race up and down. Originating from China, Dragon Boats are normally crewed by twenty-two people, one person sits at the front of the boat facing backwards and bangs on a drum to beat out the pace for the twenty forward-facing paddlers while one person stands at the rear and steers the boat. Stanley and I were left with little choice other than to watch the show, and very good it was too! The boat teams were very enthusiastic and at full tilt the boats were really powering through the water.

We spent the night moored in the city; and it was not

long before we could hear the first of the shouts and screams of the city's night-time revellers. Cat and I steeled ourselves for a long noisy night; but, to be fair, apart from the odd shouted argument, there was not too much disruption to our night's slumber.

We woke to a sunny bank holiday Monday morning and took Stanley for his walk with an ulterior motive: to see if the Severn Café was open. We were in luck, the café was just opening so we would be the first customers of the day. Cat ordered the "builders' breakfast" while I walked Stanley around the green until it was served. We did not have to wait long and once it arrived I felt full to the point of bursting just looking at it, it was massive! Both Cat and I valiantly chomped our way through, but there was no way even with Stanley's enthusiastic assistance that we would emerge victorious at the far side of the plate and we both had to admit defeat. Collecting the left-over bread to feed to the swans, we waved our thanks to the café staff with assurances that we would be back and waddled our way to *Akita*.

Swans fed, Stanley walked, watered, and satisfied with his eclectic breakfast we headed south and into Diglis Lock. It was early, the lock had just opened, and we were the first user of the day. I chatted to the keeper as the chamber emptied and he soon had us on our way south once again.

Cat took a turn at the helm and I made us both a cup of tea and sat on the foredeck to drink mine. I then nearly spilt the contents of my cup when I heard a blowing noise akin to the sound a whale makes when it surfaces; it was no whale, but it was a species that was equally out of place here miles up-river. What Cat and I had both heard from different ends of the boat was a seal!

I ran to the stern of the boat to take over at the helm so that Cat could grab her camera. Predictably the seal, who had been gallivanting on the surface, now became camera-shy and disappeared beneath the water. I let *Akita* drift on the current hoping that it would make another appearance. We were both looking over the stern rail at the river behind us – Stanley sensing our excitement had got up from his bed and was also scanning the water. The blowing noise was emitted again; but this time it was from a long way ahead of us and near the bank, either the seal had swum under *Akita*'s hull or perhaps there was more than one of them here. Cat was frustrated because she did not get a shot of the seal before it once again went into submarine mode. We waited for what seemed an age but the animal did not make another appearance. We had to assume the seal had had enough of the passing boaters behaving like paparazzi, and had decided to become a recluse.

I reluctantly pushed the throttle forward to continue our journey south, then a minute later the seal popped its head out of the water a long away from our stern, Cat managed to zoom in and get one photo before it disappeared for the last time.

Later we did some research; it turned out that the seal had been around since the floods of the previous year and although it was a female the locals had named her Keith after a Royalist commander Colonel George Keith; the colonel fought in the Battle of Worcester in 1651, however the battle did not go so well for him; he was taken prisoner and ended up in the Tower of London. Keith (the seal) was becoming quite a celebrity; but not everyone was happy with her – the "brave hunters of the deep", the Angling Trust, had apparently looked into the possibility of shooting the poor errant beast, it seems that they did not like the competition and they were worried about Keith eating all of "their" fish!

Leaving the seal to single-handedly divest the entire length of the River Severn of fish, we continued on our way south. During the trip home I was marking the locations of all the moorings along the river on the map in my waterway guide, then grading them from "good" through "not bad" to "poor". This information would be invaluable on future trips – especially in the event that we should be caught out on the river in spate or if we were delayed and then trapped by closed locks. I was also noting the locations of service stations so I could keep *Akita*'s fuel tanks topped up. My waterways guide was starting to look used and dog-eared, just like proper boaters' would be, I was becoming quite proud of it!

It was time to put the kettle on again – after all we were on a boat! Cat was at the helm so it was down to me to make the tea. I held the kettle under the tap and turned it on, water flowed then stopped, spurted, dribbled, then it refused to produce any more liquid. This was serious, I am an Englishman, I needed tea! Yet again it was my fault, I had run the water tank dry. I changed the pump from one tank to the other then turned on the tap, but nothing happened, I had killed the pump by running it dry. Totally my fault and worse still I had to tell Cat. I shouted toward the stern deck where Cat was busy steering, 'Honey, the water pump has just stopped working for no apparent reason – damn thing was brand new too! We'll have to stop at Upton to get a new one.' So I got away with that one – unless Cat reads this ...

Speed Limits

I was still in the cabin trying to think of ways cover up the fact that I was solely responsible for the broken water pump. Cat called me to the rear deck, and when I arrived she pointed forward towards a small boat that was drifting across the river. The boat had an aluminium hull that could seat two or three and was fitted with an outboard motor. There was a single occupant; a fisherman who seemed oblivious to the fact that he was drifting into the path of other boats that were cruising up and down the river. We managed to bypass him without incident and thought no more about it. Some time later, though, there was a convoy of cruisers heading in the opposite direction to us, correctly cruising on the right-hand side of the navigation. Then came the idiot. He came down-river on the wrong side; heading straight towards the convoy of boats at an incredible speed. The cruisers had to change course and scatter to avoid being hit by the buffoon in the aluminium torpedo. As he overtook us and then hurtled past the cruisers his wake hurled *Akita* and then the other boats around in the water. Looking at the faces and shaking heads in the other boats, both Cat and I could tell that the occupants were not impressed!

The only logical reason I can think of for this fool's turn of speed was that angler was losing the battle with fish; being out-numbered he was making a tactical retreat. Or maybe Keith the seal had got word about the Angling

Trust's intent to bump her off and was attempting a pre-emptive strike.

There are speed limits on the inland waterways and with good reason: going too fast and creating breaking wash against the canal/river bank will cause erosion and can damage wildlife habitat. Cruising too fast when passing other boats will upset the occupants; no one wants to spill their tea and curry stains are hard to remove from a tee shirt! If you want to go fast then the Inland Waterways Network is not the right place for you!

In general the speed limit on most canals is 4mph (a fast walking pace), though there are some exceptions to this:

The limit on the Gloucester & Sharpness Canal is 6mph.

On the River Severn the speed limit is 6mph when going up-river and 8mph when cruising down.

The limit on the River Avon is 4mph when going up-river and 6mph when cruising down.

You should check the speed limit for whatever waterway you are cruising, in any event if you are creating breaking wash against the bank you are going too fast and should slow down.

Edward Elgar (not Music to My Ears!)

Having to stop at Upton was no bad thing; Stanley had been a good boy and deserved a walk. We managed to tie to the visit mooring and clutching the old water pump (which had died for no apparent reason) we set off in search of its clone. The shop that I was hoping to obtain one from was closed, but I did manage to find some rubber sandals that I had been looking to acquire for months. Since we had the boat we were using a lot of public showers; now I would be able to have a shower without having to take my shoes off, and not risk getting a verruca or other nasty foot infection. As great as this may be, it was still not getting me any closer to getting the tap water running, and I wanted to do so before Cat started to ask awkward questions, such as, 'Did you break the pump by running it dry?'

We walked across the nice riveted river bridge to Upton Marina and were directed to the chandlery, where, after a short wait, I emerged with a new pump in a bag and less money in my pocket.

With Cat steering us south; I set about the quick job of replacing the water pump and within ten minutes the kettle was boiling water for our delayed mug of tea.

Cat, being refreshed by tea, was happy to continue at the helm so I went for a snooze. I woke just as we were approaching Mythe Bridge, surprised how far we had come and quickly called the lock-keeper to let him know we were inbound. The lock was ready so we cruised straight in. While we were locking down, the keeper advised us that the tide was running – this meant there would be a lot of debris on the river.

One of the things that really spoils the River Severn is the wooden pallets of the type used by forklift trucks that clutter the bank along the length of the river. The pallets are very unsightly and also can be a hazard for boats as quite often they are swept away from the bank and then float low in the water, unseen by the helmsman. I assume this clutter is for fishermen to sit on although to date I have not actually seen anyone doing this.

We made good time and were soon at the approach to the Upper Parting. It was time to call the Gloucester lock-keeper and he gave me the news that I did not want to hear. It had to happen sooner or later, and today would be the day that we were to meet *Edward Elgar* (the large hotel boat, not the man) and we would meet "her" on the narrowest part of the River Severn with the most twists and turns. This would be the real test of how relaxed I would be at the helm when meeting a large vessel on this part of the river. We were now in radio contact with the *Elgar*; the captain requested that we attempt to pass each other at a specific part on the river to which I agreed, but I was not sure how I was going to time it correctly. Cat went forward to keep a lookout for *Edward Elgar* and to point out the location of the large amount of debris that was now in our path. The debris ranged from wooden pallets (still without anyone sitting on them), leaves, through branches to whole trees, and the last thing we wanted was to foul the propeller with a goliath bearing down on us!

We got to the agreed location and I held *Akita* there against the current with the engine going astern, but now all the debris that we had passed was catching us up; I had to avoid it by swinging *Akita* from one side of the river to the other. *Edward Elgar* was inbound from the south and with trees floating towards us from the north it was not a great situation to be in. To my surprise though, both Cat and I were fine about it, we were relaxed, I was almost having fun! There was no wind so *Akita* was reasonably easy to control even though we were going astern against the current; all we had to do was wait for the *Elgar* to appear.

We heard her before we saw her, her horn blasted out to announce her imminent arrival. I responded by pressing *Akita*'s horn but other than a pitiful little clicking sound nothing was emitted (we would later find out that our split charger was broken so our battery had discharged), this was not a problem, using the radio I called *Edward Elgar*'s captain to let him know that we could see him. *Elgar* slowed to a stop and the captain asked me to bring *Akita* on and pass him as quickly as I could; I needed no further encouragement, pushing the throttle fully forward and, waving to the passengers and crew, we passed the stationary vessel as fast as we could before she began to drift. The captain thanked me for accommodating his request to pass on this part of the river, and we were both on our way without losing any paint.

We were still playing dodgems with the prolific debris as we approached Gloucester Lock, the keeper radioed to ask me to tie up to the chains on the wall before the lock. This was done and we had a bit of a wait while the lock was emptied. I had expected the lock to be ready because *Edward Elgar* had just locked down onto the river and the keeper knew we were inbound, but for some reason the lock had been refilled. There was a lot of debris in the river; in fact there was a tree across the lock gates. The water was ejected from the lock which seemed to flush the debris away from the gates. Later, when writing this book, I telephoned Gloucester Lock to ask about this – Mike the duty lock-keeper was very helpful and confirmed that it is an option to "scour" the lock. This is something the keepers can do but may be restricted from doing so in times of drought.

Less than a month later; Gloucester Lock was out of action for a few days because debris had become lodged in the riverside offside gate and it would not close. Divers had to be called in the clear the obstruction. Thankfully the stoppage did not occur during the weekend that we were cruising.

One thing I have noticed is that the most lock-keepers know their patch of river very well, do seem to look after the boaters cruising on their waterways, and also have their best interests at heart. The keepers always offer advice on the conditions of the river and seem happy to answer any question that you may have. Some keepers are boaters themselves so have an even greater understanding of the need of the crews navigating the waterways.

If you are contemplating cruising the potentially tricky part of the River Severn near to Gloucester; you should consider telephoning Gloucester Lock (or call them on VHF channel 74), to enquire about the condition of the river at the time you intend to be there.

As soon as the entrance to the lock was cleared, the gates were opened and we were given the green light to enter. It takes about fifteen minutes to lock up from the river and this gave me time to reflect on our trip. Both Cat and I (and Stanley) had had a great time on our few days away, Cat was so enthusiastic she was already planning a fifteen-day cruise for us that was still over a year away! We enjoyed the trip for all the usual reasons: time away from work being the main one, but there was something else underpinning the enjoyment – there was a sense of satisfaction. I think that was because we were becoming more confident boaters, we were working as a team, sharing the workload, and feeling relaxed about being on the boat. I also felt a little sad (we both did) we did not want to come home, we both just want to keep cruising our little floating home from home around the inland waterways of Britain.

Lock filled and reflection over we chugged back to our home mooring at Saul Marina. We still had another day's holiday and I did not want to leave the boat. I spent the last day of freedom from work fixing and adjusting a few things on *Akita*.

That September Feeling

On my last day before work, I had to sort out a small flooding problem in *Akita*'s gas locker. The vent hole in a boat's gas locker has to be as low as practical, this is to allow any gas that leaks from the gas cylinders to escape out of the boat (gas is heaver than air). The vent hole in *Akita* was very close to the waterline and located in the transom at the stern of the boat. The problem with this is that the bilges in the gas locker would be flooded with water every time that we reversed. I did not want to compromise boat safety by sealing the vent and cutting another hole higher up, so I installed a platform to raise up the bottles from the deck by a few centimetres to keep them out of the water in the bilges. Now most of the water could run freely back out of the boat and what little remained would evaporate over time without coming in to contact with our gas cylinders.

One of the things that both Cat and I agreed on was that the chair at the helm would have to be replaced with one with a back rest. The internet was once again trawled through and a suitable seat was ordered. The chair was delivered the very next working day and well in time for the following weekend. Saturday arrived and after Stanley took me for my morning walk I shot down to the marina to install the new seat complete with its back rest. We can now be seen cruising along the Cut in an almost reclining position, all we needed now was a loud stereo, some furry dice, and blacked-out windows, to look very cool!

I purchased a new folding sack truck; this time buying it in person from a local camping shop, so I could see exactly what I was getting for my money, and to make sure that it was robust enough to handle the weight of a full 25-litre jerrycan. The new little truck has proved to be very useful!

This now left me having to make a decision about what to do with the first truck that I had bought – apart from its problems, it was still new and I was sure that someone with the time and inclination could do something with it. At our marina there are some large waste bins and a recycling area for berth-holders to dispose of rubbish. There seems to be an unwritten/unspoken rule that if you are disposing of something that you think maybe of use to another boater, instead of putting it in the bin you place it to one side so that it can be seen and apprised by others who may have a use for it. In fact I have taken advantage of this useful system myself, when I picked up a handy bit of wood which was just right for a small project that I was working on in *Akita*. In the spirit of reciprocation, recycling, and the unwritten rule, I left the truck by the bin and then went to the loo, when I came out less than five minutes later, I saw a boater walking away happily clutching his new little sack truck – all I could do as I tried to suppress a smile was hope that he would find a cure for the rickets!

The weather had been very kind to us all summer long – almost as good as 1976. We could not have started our boating life with better weather, but it was now mid-September, the heat of the summer was dissipating, and the nights were drawing in. We would have to face up to the reality that autumn was fast approaching with cold weather in its wake. It would not be long before we would have to think about mothballing *Akita* for the long winter. The water tanks would have to be drained and the pipes run dry to avoid frost damage, and I would have to figure out what I was going to do about winterising the engine.

A gas leak or fire in a building on dry land is never a good thing, and when occurring on a boat they are especially dangerous. Gas is heavier than air and if a leak occurs on a boat the gas will sink to the bottom of the vessel and, being unable to escape, it will accumulate there waiting to ignite or suffocate an unsuspecting boater. If a fire breaks out aboard not only do you have to exit the boat you also have the added problem of getting ashore, in addition the situation is made more dangerous because the vessel will be carrying gas bottles and fuel.

On board *Akita* we have gas, smoke, and carbon dioxide detectors. These are essential and all boats should be fitted with them. However, one of the things that I had noticed when walking around the marina is a beeping sound that is emitted from the cabins of a number of boats which are left unattended for a long time. The source of the noise is smoke and carbon dioxide detectors that are beeping to indicate that they have low batteries. This noise must be irritating to other boat users, especially at night when sound easily carries across the water. With this in mind, when I close our boat down for a prolonged absence I remove the batteries from the detectors and place them in a prominent position so we do not forget to reinstall them when we return to the boat! This is a personal choice – but should you also do this you *must* remember to put the batteries back in!

With the prospect of not being able to use the boat for a while, I started to think about how the previous owner of our boat must have felt having to sell her and how hard it must have been for him to give up a life on the water. True, the vessel was in a sad state of disrepair, but if it is your boat then I guess it is your pride and joy, and having to give it up must have been a hard and sad decision for him to make, especially after owning her for eleven years!

161

With this in mind the prospect of not being able to cruise much during the coming winter months was brought into perspective and did not seem so bad. Both Cat and I were already looking forward to a full cruising season the following year, and were hoping that the summer would be as good.

The vacant moorings in the marina were now starting to fill up with boats returning after spending the summer months cruising around the Inland Waterways Network. I was still no closer to that elusive lottery win so would still have to be content with mini cruises but work aside it had been a great summer.

If You See Burt Lancaster, Ask Him if He Has My Phone

STOP PRESS, the summer is back! Good weather did not seem to want to relinquish its grip and we had two more great weekends of warm and fairly sunny September, not exactly BBQ weather but good enough to spend the weekends on the boat and take mini cruises.

It was a Saturday and I was determined to make the most of the bonus weekend of extra summer. I was making ready to take the two-hour cruise to Gloucester when Mark, from the battle-scarred boat next door, asked me if I was going north or south. I told him I was going north to do some food shopping, Mark then asked me something I never thought I would be asked: 'If you see Burt Lancaster, ask him if he has my phone.' I was a bit taken aback by this because I did not think it would be possible without the use a Ouija board; as far as I was aware Burt Lancaster died in 1994. Mark must have seen the look of confusion on my face, so he clarified his request by telling me that his friend Matt lived on *Burt Lancaster*, a narrowboat, that I would find moored somewhere along the Cut. Mark thought that he had left his mobile phone on the boat or maybe in Matt's car. I agreed that if I saw *Burt Lancaster* I would make enquiries about the missing phone.

I chugged along the G&S with Stanley snoozing on the deck at my feet, as I neared Rea Bridge I spotted *Burt*

Lancaster and pulled alongside. It must have seemed odd to the occupants to have a stranger on a boat that they did not recognise trying to get their attention – after some time Matt appeared on the foredeck from the galley, fish slice in hand to see what I wanted. After a little more confusion as to whom I was and what I wanted, Matt realised what I was going on about and promised to look for Mark's phone. He took my number and said he would call me should he find it.

I arrived at the mooring outside the superstore and tied up. After taking Stanley for a walk around the docks I grabbed some essentials and it was as I was at the checkout that Matt called to say that he had found Mark's mobile phone. It was arranged that I could pick the phone up on my way back to Saul Junction. Mark was very happy to have his phone returned!

It struck me that messages must have been passed along the canal system in this way from one boat to another for hundreds of years – if Mark had not lost his modern form of communication I would not have thought about the old. Don't get me wrong: I think contemporary communication systems are great, but I think we have lost the "contact" with people, sure we can text, email, and talk to people from any distance but if Mark had not lost his phone I would not have met Matt and not had the opportunity to have had a chat to him face to face. I am starting to like "Canal Communication": relaxed conversations that take place along the Cut, in locks or on the towpath, face to face at a slower, friendlier pace.

How Far We Have Come

The following day Cat was back on board after visiting her mum the preceding day. It was decided that we would go for a cruise again to make the most of the weather. As we were chugging along, several swans were flying towards us and then very low, right alongside our boat. They looked very elegant and for some reason they reminded me of the old Lancaster bombers of Second World War vintage and the film *The Dam Busters*. It was a great photo opportunity, if only Cat had remembered to bring her camera!

We were not the only ones who thought this was a good photo opportunity; I watched a guy on the towpath drop what he was carrying and grab his camera and hastily snap a shot of the low-flying swans. As he was reviewing his effort on the small screen on the back of his camera, I shouted across to him, 'Did you get the shot?' He replied with an affirmative smile and proud thumbs-up!

We again went to the supermarket so Cat could do the shopping: "properly this time". I waited with Stanley and the boat as Cat went in to buy food that we could "actually live on". I am not sure what Cat's problem is; I do take into consideration a balanced diet when buying food and always fill my shopping trolley with something from all of the main food groups: pizza, curry, and kebabs.

While I was waiting for Cat to do the shopping "properly" I took the opportunity to chat to a fellow boater; he was stood on the stern deck of the narrowboat *Shadowfax* that had moored up behind *Akita*. Presumably he had also been relegated to waiting on the boat for some perceived shopping misdemeanour while his better half did the job correctly. He informed me he and his wife had been living on their boat for eight years and that he could never go back to living in a house.

Cat returned to *Akita* – far too quickly to have done the shopping correctly and this was proved by the total lack of curry to be found within the carrier bags. We cast off and had an event-free but nice cruise south towards our home mooring, that is, it was event-free until we arrived back at Saul Junction Bridge.

Upon arriving we rapidly caught up with a small boat that could not have been more than 10 foot long, fitted with an outboard motor, travelling at about 1 mile an hour and zigzagging all over the Cut! The guy was working the steering wheel so fast to the left and the right that I thought he was going to have a cardiac arrest. He reminded me of my first attempt to steer *Akita* when I was continuously over-correcting, but this guy was in what amounted to no more than an oversized bath tub.

There was quite a crowd gathering to watch his progress (or lack thereof); everyone was trying to suppress their smiles as the small boat came past at a snail's pace, with *Akita* hot on its tail. There was another boat with seven or eight people aboard waiting to come through the bridge in the opposite direction and they could no longer contain their mirth and were cruelly but unavoidably laughing out loud. Cat was on the foredeck of *Akita* and she was smiling and kept looking back towards me and rolling her eyes, which only served to make me laugh even though I was trying not to be judgemental.

We turned around in the basin and unfortunately had to continue to follow the erratic boat; it took an age to get to the marina entrance where the skipper of the small boat managed to crash into the side as he attempted to enter. After extracting the boat from the side wall of the marina entrance, he then made his way towards the slipway which thankfully is in the opposite direction from our mooring. I will not say what the boat was named but it had a "3" in the title; presumably the boats with numbers "1" and "2" in their names had been sunk at an earlier date. Joking aside, watching the guy trying to steer the boat did make me realise how I must have looked when I first collected *Akita* all those months before. How far I have come in boat handling; but I must remember not to be too smug, the wind can always catch me out!

As we cruise along the Cut it is normally fairly easy to guess which boats are lived in and which are not – the boats with paraphernalia on the roof are usually frequented by "Live-aboards". The gear typically stored on top of the cabin can range from flower pots to bikes, trolleys, coal, and logs. Some people think this is scruffy but I disagree – for me the eclectic possessions just add to the cornucopia of sights that can be seen out there on the canal.

Some boats are, however, not so aesthetically pleasing, these poor unloved vessels are neglected, half-sunk and in some cases look like they have been abandoned. They have paint peeling away and are so grimy that you could not see through the windows even if you wanted to; they are effectively mini ghost ships. Unbelievably, some of these boats are lived in, the only sign of life is the tell-tale wisp of smoke rising from the flume protruding from the roof. As opposed to referring to the occupants of these boats as Live-aboards I light-heartedly refer to them as "Dead-aboards".

Avon Calling

The good weather just did not want to leave: we were truly
having an Indian summer, and by a happy coincidence I
still had some leave due me. I booked a Friday and
Monday off work so that we could have a nice long
weekend and the plan was to cruise the River Avon for a
day or two. Due to other commitments and time
constraints this would be our first opportunity to journey
along the Avon, and we were both looking forward to our
trip.

We had a pleasant Friday afternoon cruise up the River
Severn and were locked up on to the River Avon by Bob,
the ever helpful resident lock-keeper.

The River Avon is independent and administered by the
Avon Navigation Trust (ANT). ANT is a registered charity
and the navigation is run by mainly by volunteers with
only a few employees. The river was brought back from a
near derelict state in the 1950s and by 1974 was fully
navigable.

The standard Canal and River Licence will not cover
you on the River Avon. However, if you do not wish to
purchase a full year's licence for this river, you can buy
one that will allow you to cruise for 24 or 48 hours or 7,
14, or 30 days. We bought a 48-hour excursion pass from
Bob at Avon Lock. It was getting late so we moored in
Tewkesbury for the night.

The grounded narrowboat *Unicorn* was still sitting at a

crazy angle on top of the wall and was starting to look very scruffy. There was also a small boat that had sunk in the river just below the precariously placed narrowboat. I wondered how long it would be before these eyesores would be removed?

Stanley was taken for a well-deserved walk, then I was despatched to get a pizza and some chicken wings for our evening meal. After dinner was consumed it was time to take Stanley out for the last time. Although it was dark I could tell the poor lad was not himself and this became more obvious once we were back in the light aboard *Akita*. In case of further deterioration, and just to be of the safe side, we went online and found the telephone number of the local vet before settling down for the night. The next morning Stanley seemed to have rallied a bit so we left our mooring and headed up-river, passing under King John's Bridge.

King John's Bridge is constructed of four stone brick arches; the largest and navigable right-hand arch at an offset angle; I had to swing over to the centre of the navigation and then cut back across the river in order to line *Akita* up to pass cleanly through the bridge. As the sign instructed, I gave a long blast on the horn to warn any oncoming boats before passing through the structure. When we cruised under the bridge I noticed the grooves that have been worn in the brickwork above my head by vessels over the years (check your air draft!)

Once we were through the bridge the river opened out and we passed through Tewkesbury Marina – the marina has nearly four hundred flood-protected moorings for boats within the marina basin and also on the river-side itself. There were many different types of craft moored here ranging from small speedboat/cruisers and sailing boats through narrowboats to large expensive cruisers. There was plenty to distract us as we went through the marina facilities.

Although the Avon empties into the Severn, the two rivers could not be more different; to my mind the River Severn is more industrial, you seem to be hemmed in by the high banks and the trees that grow on them, and the Severn is the equivalent to a motorway. The Avon, however, is a much prettier river, the banks are lower, and you are afforded a better view of the surrounding area. He Avon is more akin to a scenic route on a countryside road.

Although the Avon is very pretty it should be treated with respect; it can change from a relatively tranquil flow to a most difficult navigation in the event of heavy or extended rainfall, even in the summer months. Like the River Severn the Avon has "automatic flood warning signs" located near to the exit of most locks; these are basically coloured boards placed at river level:

If the water is in the green zone this indicates normal level/safe conditions.

If the water is in the amber zone this indicates increased current; you can proceed with caution but you may want to find a flood safe mooring as soon as possible.

If the water is in the red zone this indicates danger and you should stop and moor!

If you are in any doubt about the river conditions, or would like to enquire about them before you commit to cruising on the river, you can call the helpful Avon Lock keeper. ANT also have webcams at strategic place along the length of the river so you can see the state of the river for yourself online.

As we locked on to the River Avon we were given a very handy "welcome information" guide; this gave advice on the river including the above flood warning and also where the flood-safe moorings are. While we were at the Avon Lock we also purchased the informative *Navigation & Visitors Guide* for the River Avon that the ANT has published.

Once we had cruised past the marina we were into open

countryside and both Cat and I liked the river straight away; it was good to be back out on the water and exploring a part of the waterways network that was new to us! After nearly three miles we approached the M5 bridge. I have driven over this bridge at breakneck speed with the rest of the rat race more times than I would care to admit. As I drove over the bridge I always wondered what it would be like to be in a boat on the river and now I know: it is very nice indeed! Once again I was struck by the way that your perception is altered when you view the scenery from a totally different perspective (and speed) afforded you by being on the waterway – my assessment on this day: waterway slow but good, Motorway fast but bad!

If anything the landscape became even nicer the further up-river we went; we soon arrived at the first river lock that we would have to operate on our own. The gates were open so we cruised straight into Stensham Lock. Cat held the ropes to secure *Akita* to the wall while I operated the lock. This was the easiest lock that I have had to operate so far, the paddles were easy to wind up and down and even though the gates were large they seemed light when I had to open or close them, and so we were soon on our way again.

To our surprise the river was even better once we were through the lock; after just over two miles further on we came to the "Swan's Neck" (think hairpin bend) as we chugged around what seemed like a never-ending curve I reflected once again that a few short months ago I would have been worried about meeting another boat coming down-river in the opposite direction, but now I almost relished the prospect.

Avon Abort

As we had been cruising we were keeping an eye on Stanley, who was clearly not happy. As much as we were enjoying our cruise along the Avon we had to think about our poor boy. Even though we had the contact details of a vet in the area we wanted to take Stanley to our local vet's for continuity of care, so as we approached Nafford Lock we reluctantly decided that we would have to turn about and head for home.

It was a real shame this was perhaps the last chance that we would have to cruise on the Avon this year; the navigation was getting better and better and we were really enjoying the cruise and the prospect of spending another night out on the river, but Stanley was our responsibility and he had to come first.

I turned *Akita* around just before the lock and we started heading back down-river. Cat took over steering while I did some calculations to see if it would be possible to get back to Gloucester Docks before the locks on the River Severn were closed for the night.

By my reckoning we would be able to make it back to Gloucester in time. Bob the Avon lock-keeper was surprised to see us back so soon until we explained about Stanley. There was another boat called *Ripple* waiting to lock down, but the owner very kindly offered to let us go first. Bob soon had us on our way and even informed the keeper at the next lock that we would encounter on the

River Severn that we were on our way and had an ailing dog aboard.

The journey on the Severn "motorway" did not seem to take that long at the breath-taking speed of 6mph that *Akita* can achieve when going down-river, and we were back at the docks well before the lock closed for the day. I caught the bus home, picked up the car, and was back at the docks within 45 minutes to collect Cat and dog.

We took poor Stanley to the vet's out of hours service; and after prodding, poking, and an invasive procedure that involved a loss of Stanley's dignity, a thermometer, and a very shocked dog, our poor boy was diagnosed as having a bladder infection. Two injections and a small fortune later we returned home to wait and see what the results of this endeavour would bring in the morning.

I had a sleepless night due to Stanley's snoring, but he had a great night's rest. They do say that sleep is the best medicine and in the morning he was a much happier boy.

Akita was still moored at the docks; so Cat gave me a lift so that I could chug the boat back to our home moorings. The weather was still great so I was happy to sit on the foredeck and chat to the guy on a neighbouring narrowboat, *Mystic Lady*. We talked about the changes that had taken place on the waterway network since he started cruising in the 1970s, the lock and bridge closing times, and anything to do with boats. The time flew by, mugs of tea were drunk, and I was shocked to realise that it was now mid-afternoon; I would have to get going! Even though it was the last weekend in September the sun was shining so I took the opportunity to lower the roof for the cruise back to our home port.

Once I had secured *Akita* to our mooring, I put the kettle on then went out to the foredeck to sit in the sun; Mark was sitting Buddha-like on top of his boat sunning himself and he recounted his tale of woe. Apparently he had been drinking with Matt (from the *Burt Lancaster*) at

The Pilot, a pub that is popular with boaters due to its proximity to the canal (you will find it near to Sellar's Bridge). The way Mark tells it is that they were both very drunk, the pair had taken Matt's small tender boat to get to the pub; and had spent the evening getting very merry. They left the establishment and due to their inebriated state Mark had to 'help Matt into the small boat'. Once Matt was safely installed Mark then leant across to get into the boat himself but missed his handhold and fell head-first into the Cut, going straight under the boat to emerge somewhat more sober on the other side.

From time to time you do hear that someone has fallen in to the Cut, more often than not alcohol was in part something to do with the navigational error that resulted in the soaking. Although at the time of writing it is not illegal to be drunk in charge of a private boat, you have to ask yourself about the merits or otherwise of being so. If you ask me water and vast amounts of alcohol are like water and oil they just don't mix! (Sorry, Mark!)

Cat arrived that afternoon with Stanley in tow; we took him for a gentle walk around the marina before setting down for our evening curry. We reflected on how nice the River Avon had been and how we were keen to cruise the full length of the navigation; we vowed to return as soon as possible, even if that proved to be the following year!

Mooring

Near to the start of this book I mentioned that I did not know where I was allowed to moor, so I thought I would include a bit about mooring here. This is not meant to be a definitive guide (I am not the authority on this) but I thought it would be useful to give you the information from this boater's perspective and how I understand it.

On most canals, unless otherwise stated, you can pretty much moor anywhere along the towpath side that you like for up to fourteen days. There are, however, some obvious exceptions to this, you should not stop at a water or pump-out point for longer than it takes you to use the facilities, likewise you should not moor at winding points (turning points) or near to junctions, or blind bends, etc.

Some moorings along the Cut are "long-term moorings" this means the boat owners have paid to moor there long-term and they use these places as their home mooring. These will be marked (look for the long-term mooring signs). Long-term moorings should be treated like a private mooring and you should not stop there even if they appear vacant.

Other mooring sites will have time restrictions – two examples of this would be the "visitor mooring" on the pontoons at Gloucester Docks, these are restricted to 48 hours and the moorings immediately outside the supermarket near to High Orchard Bridge are only 4 hours! Where there are restrictions in place there is normally a sign to give you the information that you will need.

When you are mooring at popular spots, or on the limited flood-safe river moorings that are available, you should always consider other boaters. When you find a spot, moor as close as practical to other boats so that the available mooring space is used efficiently (watch out for the other boats' rudders/stern-drives/outboards). You should also be prepared to move your boat along a bit in order to fill gaps as appropriate.

If you have to use mooring stakes, try to put a reflective/bright marker on them, even if this is just a carrier bag, to stop people tripping over them.

Always try to loop back and tie off to the dolly or mooring cleat aboard your boat; this is done to dissuade foolish people undoing your mooring lines! (Vandals will not be so keen to step on to your boat to untie a knot!) If you are concerned that someone might undo your mooring lines and set you adrift; you can always lower your anchor over the side; this will at least stop you drifting far.

One last thing, albeit an obvious one; never stretch your mooring lines over the towpath; I have seen this done and it is interesting to see the reaction of walkers, runners, and cyclists!

Summer is Finally Over, but What a Way to Go!

I was getting withdrawal symptoms, but as I was still getting my fix of curry it could only be down to one thing: I was missing the boat! It was mid-October and I had not used the boat for a week or two so I drove down to the marina just to step onboard and to check *Akita* over. Of course once I was aboard I could not help myself, and before I knew it I was chugging up the Cut and soon found my way to Gloucester Docks. I got a takeaway and sat in the cabin to eat while watching the world go by. To my surprise, and contrary to the weather forecast; the sun put in an appearance and it soon became warm enough to sit out on deck. This would prove to be one of the last salvos of sun in the dying Indian summer: a summer that we would mourn the passing of, for it had been with us for so long we would miss it like a dear departed friend!

I knew that the sun could not last and the weather report for the following day was atrocious; so with heavy heart I decided to make my way back to the marina, after all this mini cruise was just a bonus! The *Queen Boadicea II* was just about to make her way under Llanthony Bridge, so to save the bridge having to open again just for me, I quickly radioed the bridge-keeper and then followed the *QB2* out of the docks.

I was three-quarters of the way back when the sky went from blue to grey to black and then came the rain, thunder, and lightning. It rained so hard that it came through the air vents in the roof and the thunder could be heard over the noise of the engine! I could not see a thing and had to slow down so that I was barely making any headway. I knew that I should stop but to do so would mean having to get out of the boat to tie it to the side and I would have been socked to the skin in an instant.

I turned on the navigation lights (I was so pleased that I installed them) and slowly made my way down the Cut with eyes straining to see through the windscreen (I really should look into getting a wiper fitted!). I was held by a red light at Parkend Bridge so that the Waterways Museum's large passenger cruiser, *King Arthur*, could come through. I was pleased I met *King Arthur* here, where the canal is wider and that we were both going slower, at least we could see each other through the storm! *King Arthur* passed me and *Akita* was rocking in her wake as I made my way south through the bridge.

The storm stopped as quickly as it had started, and as I turned around in the Saul Junction Basin, the sky above me was clear blue, I looked back towards the north and the direction of the storm. Junction Bridge and the picturesque keeper's cottage were framed by a picture-perfect rainbow, in fact the best rainbow that I have ever seen; I could almost believe that there would be a pot of gold at each end!

Time to Feed the Ducks

I have itchy feet and when on the boat I like to be on the move. I am sure if I had more free time I would be prepared to stop in one place to admire the view and just relax, but there is something in me that keeps driving me forward. Other people seem to be happy to take time off work to do nothing; they are content to just lounge about, soak up the sun and have a drink. That is fine for others but is just not for me. I have to be doing something, to achieve something or I feel my limited free time away from the office has been wasted. When I was working on the boat I was happy enough to stay put – I could not cruise but at least I was being productive. I knew that each little job completed was a step forward to being able to use the boat for cruising.

However, sometimes I am forced in to inactivity; it is rare, I grant you that, but it does happen. There is the odd occasion when there are no little jobs to do aboard *Akita*, and I cannot leave wherever I am because Cat is away from the boat and I am waiting for her to return. Stanley will have just had a good walk and is lazily sprawled on the deck and would not be too impressed (or accommodating) if I tried to get him to move, so I am effectively redundant. This is the time I reach for the stale bread, the fresh bread, or even Cat's secret stash of Jacob's Cream Crackers that I am not supposed to know about.

Ducks are amazing. They can almost sense a piece of bread that has been dropped into the water at a thousand metres, they will soon make their way towards the stern of your boat to partake of a free meal. Where there is one duck, others are sure to follow and swans will not be far behind! I have been lucky enough to have swans take titbits straight from my hand – although sometimes they do get it wrong and grab my finger or thumb.

What's in a Name?

When I am able to cruise or even just walk along the Cut, one of the things I like to do is look at the other boats. I never get bored – there are so many different types to look at: small cruisers to full-length barges and all the variations of each type of boat in between will keep me intrigued throughout the day. I like to see and assess any changes or improvement that may have been made to a vessel. These modifications will sometimes give me ideas for the future: solar panels, wind turbines, or cratch covers (a cover for the foredeck) or an inventive way to carry a bike, all are filed away to be use on some possible project in the future. But what I like looking for most is the names of boats.

When Cat and I bought our boat there was the obvious discussion about the name of our new vessel; my first suggestion was "Truth over Bullshit" but Cat quickly vetoed this pithy name, my second option was "Function over Form" but this too was rejected. *Akita* was understandably the first name that we both quickly agreed on. Boat names vary from the mundane to the hilarious, from descriptive to thought-provoking. Some names obviously mean something personal to the owners, while others are making a statement. But without a doubt the best name for a narrowboat that I have seen so far and which for me summed up what life on the water is all about is: *Moor and Peace*.

Not the Weather for Boating!

Still having a few days holiday left, Dave B. and I decided that we would have a blokes' long weekend on the boat. Thursday afternoon arrived and I took *Akita* up to Gloucester Docks in readiness to lock down onto the Severn and then lock up onto the Avon, the plan was to see how far we could get along the Avon in the little time that we had. Unfortunately the rain had other ideas and the rivers were in flood, so we were unable to lock down onto the Severn on the Friday morning as planned, this meant that we were stuck on the G&S Canal. As Dave B had not cruised the full length of the canal this was no bad thing, so we set off south in the direction of Sharpness Docks. As we chugged along the rain came pouring down so my newly "installed" windscreen wiper was put to good use – I say installed, but the installation of the wiper was hardly a feat of mechanical engineering:

Step one: Purchase an old windscreen wiper from a car breaker's yard.

Step two: Bend windscreen wiper arm over the top on windscreen so that wiper is on the outside, and wiper arm is on the inside to use as a manual handle to operate wiper.

Step three: Use wiper to clear water from windscreen – simple but effective!

Four mugs of tea, several mini chocolate rolls, and some sixteen miles, later; we arrived at the Sharpness visitor moorings in time for a late lunch. Once we had moored we had our first curry of the trip: chicken curry and Bombay potatoes from a can – not too bad! We decided to have a walk round and try and find the very large Sharpness Lock. The rain had relented, but fearing that the weather was just trying the lull us into a false sense of security we took raincoats just to be on the safe side.

I had thought that our boat was rare, but as we walked along the towpath and through Sharpness Marina, I spotted amongst the diverse collection of boats two that were very similar to *Akita*; I even saw a half size version (very cute)!

The towpath came to an end just after the marina, so we followed an ascending track through some trees and emerged onto a windswept grassy hillside overlooking the canal and the industrial dockside. From our vantage point on the hill we could still see no towpath alongside the canal through the Sharpness quayside, so we followed a little-used road through a desolate landscape until we came to an establishment that at one time would have been the local post office but was now simply known as the "Dock Shop". This was the only shop in the area so we decided to go in to ask for directions. For me it was like going into a time-warp and I found myself back in the seventies. The confectionery was displayed on a sloping shelf that made up part of the shop's counter, and some of the sweets I had not seen since the aforementioned decade. Feeling bad about that fact that I had only come in to ask for directions, and seeing that there was a distinct possibility that we were the only customers of the day, and possibly of the last month or two, I thought I had better buy something! I purchased some milk, and as I was now feeling nostalgic for the seventies of my youth, I also purchased some sweets. I paid for the items from my pocket money and asked for direction toward Sharpness Lock. The lady in the shop was very helpful and we were soon trudging our way towards the lock munching our sweeties as we went.

We arrived at Sharpness Lock and we were shocked by the sheer size of it; to me it looked like the whole of Gloucester Docks would fit into the chamber with room to spare! My first thought was that *Akita* would be lost in there, should we ever decide to lock onto the River Severn to continue south toward Bristol and the Avon and Kennet Canal. This was a trip that both Cat and I were keen to do at some stage. But now looking at the size of the lock and the flow of the River Severn beyond, it seemed a little daunting.

We retreated from the lock and made our way back to *Akita* for a mug of tea, just as the kettle was boiling the rain started yet again; time for the second curry of the day!

When we woke the following morning, and because this was Dave's first night on the boat, I asked him how he had slept, 'Not well,' was his answer. 'I was a bit cold, I only had a blanket to put over me,' he explained.

'That's a shame, there's lots of bedding underneath your bed,' I said, 'perhaps I should have told you that last night'? I asked.

'Good to know!' he replied.

With drizzle still in the air and little more to hold our attention in Sharpness we chugged back up to Gloucester Docks for a very good all-day breakfast at The Barge Restaurant (situated near to the "Barge Arm" in the docks). That evening we met up with Stanley and Cat. Once Stanley had had his walk we all had a curry before Cat and Dog departed, leaving Dave and I to settle down to watch a film aboard *Akita*.

During the night the wind had really picked up, *Akita* was being pitched about on her moorings, and it was pouring with rain. I could not get to sleep because I was worried that the bridges would remain closed due to the high wind, which would trap *Akita* in the docks. Thankfully the wind had subsided a bit the following morning. As soon as it was time for the bridges to start operating I called Llanthony on the radio, the keeper said they were open for now but were keeping a close eye on the wind. As soon as Dave had finished his breakfast of reheated curry we got underway.

During the trip back to Saul Marina the wind again picked up; and by the time we were approaching Junction Bridge it felt like the wind was at storm force. I radioed the bridge-keeper earlier than I normally would have, and explained that I was struggling to control the boat in the blustery weather. It was hard to hear the reply over the roar of the wind but the bridge-keeper was a fellow boater and understood that I would not be able to hold the boat steady if I had to wait for the bridge to swing aside. The efficient keeper had the bridge open and the green light showing well before I would have had to slow down, which was a big relief.

I began my turn in the exposed basin and the full force of the wind was a little frightening as I watched it bend the whip aerial on the front of the cabin roof fully over. As soon as *Akita* was broadside to the wind the hull was flung around at an alarming rate and we were then committed to try a turn into the Stroud Water Canal.

I sent Dave to the foredeck with a fender on a length of rope to soften the impact that surely must follow as I attempted to turn into the Stroud Water Canal. As luck would have it, and with lots of steering and fine control of the throttle, I managed to get through the gap into the canal without even scraping the side, I got a thumbs-up from the bridge-keeper who was braving the weather to watch the show. I must confess I did feel quite proud of myself. Any self-congratulation was to be short-lived as I would have to tackle the next challenge of getting through the narrow marina entrance with the full force of the wind trying to keep me out.

Again my luck held and *Akita* made it into the marina basin without an impact. As I turned to line up with our berth on the far side of the basin, I watched the wind attempting to rip the flags from their poles and saw the spray blowing from the crest of the waves. I knew that there was no chance of getting into our mooring, we would simply be blown clear across the marina to impact broadside-on on other boats. I could not delay any more, I would have to make a decision within a second or two or I would start to drift.

It really was very simple – there was no choice. I would have to leave the marina basin and attempt to moor out on the canal – simple decision to make, not so easy to implement! Surprisingly, I again managed to turn around and make it back out onto the canal without colliding with the marina entrance.

Once back on the Stroud Water Canal, I aimed at the side of the Cut and against the wind and virtually rammed the bow into the side. Dave stepped onto the bank with a rope and another boater materialised to lend a hand. I threw the new helper a rope, then stepped onto the bank with yet another line and between the three of us we pulled and then tied *Akita* to the bank using a combination of mooring stakes, bollards, and piling chains. By the time we had finished Houdini could not have escaped!

The following day the news was reporting that trees had been blown down in the storm and were blocking roads, and roofs had been ripped from buildings. We did not know it at the time but this storm would be the precursor of a long winter that brought forth destructive gales; it would prove to be the wettest winter on record, resulting in prolonged flooding across the country.

I was pleased with the way I had handled the boat in the very strong wind; there was no way I could have even got the boat back along the cut as a fledgling boater of five months before, but I was still learning lessons. If you know you are going to struggle to moor or get into a specific location, have an alternative plan in place before you find yourself drifting out of control while you try to figure out what to do next.

Why Do We Keep a Boat?

Why do we keep a boat? It is a good question but it is hard to explain! I know that I have chosen to write this book, therefore you should rightly expect me to be able to put it into words, but it is not as easy as that. If I thought about it in purely logical terms then perhaps a boat would not be the most practical thing to have as a toy.

Sure, if you reside on a boat it can be a very nice and economical way to live. However, having a canal boat as a toy to use on weekends and the odd day off work and then only usually during the spring and summer, and then only if we are lucky enough to have good summer – it's an expensive pastime.

Surely a campervan would be a better prospect, you might think – they can go anywhere on the road system, which is far more extensive than the inland waterways has ever been. If the van will fit on your drive then you will not need to pay for it to be stored and road tax is still a lot cheaper than river and canal licences. Furthermore you can go where you like when you like and you can get there in quick time. None of this can be said for a boat!

With all of this undeniable logic, why would we still want to keep a boat on the water that can perhaps only be used for half of the year? I could tell you that we like to be on the water, or that we are an island race that have always had an affinity with the water, or that we like the views from the water, or that we are trying to get in touch with our inner amphibian, or several other inane reasons that I could pull out of the air to justify having a boat. But in truth I still cannot give you single good reason – but think about this: we have a campervan and still spend more time on the boat!

Even with all of the good and logical reasons for not having a boat, we still want to keep hold of *Akita* – that should tell you all you need to know: we just love it! So there it is in four little words: "we just love it"!

Akita's emblem (painted by Graham Rolfe)

Other Accent Press titles

 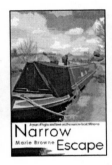 

For more information about **Michael I Rolfe**

and other **Accent Press** titles

please visit

www.accentpress.co.uk

CPSIA information can be obtained at www.ICGtesting.com
Printed in the USA
LVOW11s1545050914

402653LV00001B/35/P